HIPPOCRENE PRACTICAL

ENGLISH-HEBREW HEBREW-ENGLISH CONVERSATIONAL DICTIONARY

Romanized

David C. Gross

Newly Revised

HIPPOCRENE BOOKS
New York

For information, contact:
HIPPOCRENE BOOKS, INC.
171 Madison Avenue
New York, NY 10016

ISBN 0-7818-0137-0

Printed in the United States of America.

INTRODUCTION

How to use this book

Welcome to the world of Hebrew!

Think of it — with a little effort, you will soon be able to understand a modest amount of spoken Hebrew, and you will also be able to communicate in this ancient language, the language of the Bible.

★ ★ ★

At first glance, Hebrew looks forbidding — to westerners. After all, the alphabet is so very different-looking, and it is read and written from right to left. What's more there are no capitals, only one size of consonant — and the vowels, when they are used, are placed below, above or alongside the consonants.

And the first time you hear Hebrew — all those guttural sounds! And all those "ts" sounds. And not even a single "w" or "th" is ever used.

And yet, in all candor and honesty, Hebrew — once you put your mind to it — is easy. Yes, easy! It is a very precise, almost mathematical language, with very definite rules and regulations, which after a time become easy to follow.

The book you hold in your hand however has no Hebrew per se. Yes, there are some 7,000 Hebrew words transliterated and translated — from English to Hebrew and from Hebrew to English — but you won't find anything in the Hebrew alphabet. To encourage you to take one step at a time, the *Hebrew* in the Hebrew *alphabet* is omitted — but once you have learned a basic vocabulary, then the next logical step would be to tackle the original Hebrew alphabet, and build from there.

So, for the hundreds of thousands of visitors who come to Israel every year, for students, businessmen, for just about anyone who wishes to acquire a basic knowledge of Hebrew the easy way — here is the book for you.

A few rules to remember

1. There are quite a few guttural sounds in Hebrew, as in the German word "ach" — sound it out, get used to it, and soon you will find it quite routine.

2. Another sound that is heard often in Hebrew is the "ts" as in *fits* or *gets*.

3. The following vowel sounds are transliterated as shown:

> a as in the word *father*
> e as in the word *bell*
> i as in the word *mitt*
> o as in the word *more*
> u as in the word *push*

In addition, there are some words with the following vowels:

> ee as in *feel*
> oo as in *food*
> ai as in *main*
> eye as in *my*

A few more simple things to remember in this book:

Every vowel should be sounded.

All verbs (marked v.) are in the infinitive — to run, to eat, etc.

Most words used are nouns; those that are clearly adjectives or adverbs appear without any additional indications. Those words, however, that may be confused with another meaning are marked "adj." or "adv." for adjective or adverb respectively.

And finally: the letter g in English can either be pronounced as a hard g (as in "guard") or a soft g (as in "gist") when they are followed by e or i. Since all the g sounds in Hebrew are hard (as in "guard"), an extra u has been put in, after the g, if an e or i follow. Thus, for example, the well-known southern desert of Israel, the Negev, which also means south, has been transliterated as ne'guev.

* * *

The first half of the book, English-Hebrew, follows the alphabet, from a to z. The second half, Hebrew-English, follows the same alphabet but with a few exceptions: you will not find F, J, Q, W or X. You will find CH after B, and TS after T.

In pronouncing the Hebrew words, most two-syllable words are accented on the second syllable. For example, the well-known word for peace, *sha'lom*, should be sounded *sha'LOM*, and not SHA'lom. After a while, it will become automatic.

You will also find the overwhelming majority of Israelis happy to explain a word or give you a word if you need one. Since so many people in Israel are themselves immigrants, it is quite de rigueur for people to ask one another for linguistic help.

And don't hesitate to tell Israelis to speak more slowly if you wish to try to understand them better. Hebrew is often spoken at a too rapid-fire rate, and a request that someone speak *l'at l'at* (slowly) generally produces a smile, apology and a slowdown.

Step right in—and start talking Hebrew!

Obviously, in a small conversational dictionary like the one you are now holding, it is not possible to go into all the fine points of mastering Hebrew. It takes a long time to understand the plural endings (masculine and feminine), conjugation, declension, tenses. But it is possible to understand and make yourself understood, with the help of this concise guide to Hebrew.

The word for I is *a'nee*, pronounced a 'NEE. Suppose you wish to say, "I want to drink coffee." Here's how you would do that:

A'nee ro'tse lish'tot ka'fe.

(If you're feminine, you would change *ro'tse* to *ro'tsa*).

There are many single words that you will soon know well:

Ken (yes). *Lo* (no). *U'leye* (maybe). *To'da* (thanks). *B'va'ka'sha* (please). *S'lee'cha* (pardon). *Ka'ma?* (how much?) *Ai'fo?* (where?) *Yo'ter mi'deye* (too much).

A'nee lo ro'tse (I don't want).

A'leye la'le'chet (I have to go).

Ma shlom'cha? (how are you?)

Aich ko'r'eem l'cha? (what's your name?)

Yesh lee (I have). *Ain lee* (I don't have).

Ma ha'sha'a? (what time is it?)

Na'eem m'od (nice meeting you).

* * *

A'nee m'a'chel la'chem hats'la'cha—I wish you success.

* * *

From the time the Jews were exiled from their homeland by the Romans some two thousand years ago, Hebrew ceased being used as a daily language, but it remained in full use in the prayer book and Bible, a language for study and contemplation. About a century ago, a major effort was launched to revive the language, and to use it to help unify the Jewish communities who were gradually returning to their old-new homeland. The campaign succeeded beyond the wildest dreams of its chief motivator, Eliezer Ben Yehuda. Hebrew is taught today on college campuses throughout the western world; it is the daily language of some five million people in Israel, both Jews and non-Jews; and it is a language that is constantly being updated, as it reaches into its biblical roots to find ancient terms for modern concepts.

In the early years of America, even before the Revolutionary War against Britain, Hebrew was taught at the embryonic colleges like Harvard and Columbia. And there was even some talk among the Founding Fathers of making Hebrew the national language of the new United States.

★ ★ ★

I feel certain that this book will introduce a whole new dimension to its user. When an Israeli learns that a visitor is trying to master his language, it often happens that barriers fall, and new levels of understanding emerge.

Shalom!

— D.C.G.

A

abdomen	be'ten	advertise (v.)	par'sem; ho'dee'a
ability	ki'sharon	advertisement	mo'da'a
abnormal	lo-normalee; lo-ta'keen	advice	aitsa
		affidavit	hoda'a b'shvu'a
accent	miv'ta	affiliation	kesher
accident	t'una	affluence	she'fa
accomplish(v.)	ba'tse'a	afraid	cho'shesh
account	cheshbon	after	acha'rai
accountant	ro'e cheshbon	afterlife	o'lam ha'ba
accurate	na'chon	afternoon	acha'rai tso'ho'reye'eem
ache	k'ev		
acquaintance	ma'kar	again	shuv; od pa'am
action	p'ula	against	ne'gued
actor	sa'cha'kan	age	gueel
actual	ma'mashee	age (v.)	l'haz'keen
adage	pit'gam	agency	soch'nut
adapt (v.)	ha't'em	agenda	seder ha'yom
add (v.)	ho'sif	agent	so'chen
address	k'tovet	aggravate (v.)	l'har'gueez
adieu!	l'hit-ra'ot!	agnostic	ko'fer
administrator	m'na'hel	agree	l'haskeem
admire (v.)	ho'kir	agriculture	chak'la'ut
admission	ho'da'a	aid (v.)	la'azor
admittance	k'nisa	airconditioner	maz'gan
adult	m'vugar	airplane	ma'tos
advancement	hit'kad'mut	airport	s'de n'cheeta; n'mal t'ufa
advantage	yitron		

air mail   **arm**

air mail	do'ar aveer	announcement	hoda'a
a la	l'fee	annual	sh'na'tee
alarm	a'zaka	answer	t'shuva
alarm clock	sh'on a'zaka	anxious	do'eg
alert	er	anyone	mi'she'hu
alias	shem ba'du'ee	anyway	b'chol mik're
alien	zar	apartment	deera
alive	cheye	appeal	ba'kasha
allergy	a'ler'guee'ya	appearance	mar'e
almond	sha'ked	appendix	tosaftan
almost	kim'at	appetite	te'a'von
alms	tsedaka	hearty	b'te'a'von!
alone	l'vad; bo'ded	appetite!	
aloud	b'kol	applause	m'chee'at
also	gam		ka'pa'yeem
alternative	b'raira	apple	ta'pu'ach
altitude	go'va	apple sauce	re'sek
altogether	l'gam'rai		tapucheem
alumnus	bo'guer	appliance	mach'sheer
always	ta'meed	(electrical)	chashma'lee
ambassador	shag'reer	appointment	p'gueesha
amount (total)	sach ha'kol	appraisal	ha'aracha
amulet	ka'me'a	appropriate	mat'eem
amusement	bi'dur	approval	i'shur
ancestry	mo'tsa	apricot	mish'mesh
ancient	a'teek	apron	si'nor
angel	ma'lach	Arab	a'ravee
anger	ka'as	Arabic	a'raveet
animal	cha'ya	architect	adree'chal
ankle	kar'sol	argue (v.)	l'hit'va'kai'ach
anniversary	yom shana	argument	vi'ku'ach
wedding	ta'areech	arm	z'ro'a
anniversary	n'su'im		

2

armor	shir'yon	attitude	yachas
army	tsa'va	attorney	o'rech-deen
arrange (v.)	l'sa'der	audience	tsibur
arrive (v.)	l'ha'guee'a	auditorium	u'lam
art	o'manut		hatsa'got
artery	o'rek	aunt	do'da
artist	o'man	authentic	a'mee'tee
ascent	a'li'ya	automobile	m'cho'neet
ask (v.)	lish'ol; l'va'kesh	autumn	s'tav
asleep	ya'shen	avenue	r'chov; s'de'ra
assembly	ki'nus	average	m'mutsa
assignment	taf'keed	awaken (v.)	l'o'rer
assistant	o'zer	award	p'ras
association	chevra	awful	a'yom
assortment	miv'char	ax	gar'zen,
attache	nis'pach		kar'dom
attack	hat'kafa	axle	se'ren

3

B

baby	ti'nok	barrier	mich'shol
bachelor	ra'vak	basement	mar'tef
back	gav	bashful	beye'shan
(of person)		basin	ki'yor
back-	sheshbesh	basket	sal
gammon		bathtub	ambat'ya
bad	ra	bathing suit	be'gued yam
bag	sak	battery	so'l'la
baggage	miz'va'dot	bazaar	shuk
bake (v.)	le'efot	beach	chof
bakery	migda'ni'ya,	bead	cha'ruz
	ma'a'fee'ya	beadle	sha'mash
balcony	mir'pe'set	bean	pol
bald	ka'rai'ach	beard	za'kan
ball	ka'dur	beautiful	ya'fe (m.),
baseball	ka'dur ba'sees		ya'fa (f.)
basketball	ka'dur sal	beauty	yo'fee
soccer	ka'dur re'guel	beauty parlor	mis'para
bandage	tach'bo'shet	bed	mi'ta
banquet	mish'te	bedroom	cha'dar she'na
barber	sa'par	bee	d'vora
barefooted	ya'chef	beef	b'sar ba'kar
bareheaded	guilu'ee rosh	beer	beer'a
bargain	m'tsee'a	beet	se'lek
bargain (v.)	l'hit'ma'kai'ach	beggar	po'shet yad
barley	s'ora	beginner	ma't'cheel
barrel	cha'veet	beginning	ha't'chala

4

behavior   **brake**

behavior	hit'na'ha'gut	blister	a'va'bu'a
belief	e'muna	blood	dam
bell	pa'a'mon	blouse	chul'tsa
bellman	ka'taf	blue	ka'chol
belongings	cha'fa'tseem	blush	l'has'meek
beloved	a'huv (m.),	boarding	pen'see'yon
	a'huva (f.)	house	
below	l'mata	boat	s'feena
belt	cha'gora	body	guf
bench	saf'sal	boil (v.)	l'har'tee'ach
benevolence	che'sed	bomb	p'tsa`tsa
bent	a'kom	bone	e'tsem
bequest	y'ru'sha	book	se'fer
berry	gar'guer	book (v.)	l'hazmeen
beside	al'yad	boot	ma'gaf
best	ha'tov	borrow (v.)	lish'ol; lil'vot
	b'yo'ter	boss	m'na'hel
better	yo'ter tov	both	ha'sh'neye'-
beverage	mash'ke		yeem
bicycle	of'neye'eem	bother (v.)	l'hat'ree'ach
big	ga'dol	bottle	bak'buk
bill (account)	chesh'bon	boundary	g'vul
bird	tsi'por	bowl	k'ara
birthday	yom hu'ledet	box	kufsa
biscuit	u'guee'ya	box office	kupa
bitter	mar	boy	ye'led
black	sha'chor	boy scout	tso'fe
blanket	s'meecha	bracelet	tsa'meed
bleed (v.)	l'dam'dem	brag (v.)	l'hit'pa'er
blemish	mum	braid	tsama
blessing	b'racha	brain	mo'ach
blind	i'ver	brake	be'lem;
			ma'atsor

5

branch (on tree)   **buyer**

English	Hebrew	English	Hebrew
branch (on tree)	a'naf	bruise	cha'bura
brassiere	cha'zee'ya	brush	miv'reshet
brave	a'meets	toothbrush	mivreshet-shee'neye'eem
bread	le'chem	bud	nits'an
breakfast	a'ruchat-bo'ker	budget	tak'tseev
breath	n'sheema	buffet	miz'non
bride	ka'la	bugle	cha'tso'tsra
bridegroom	cha'tan	build (v.)	liv'not
bridge	gue'sher	building	binyan
brief	ka'tsar	bulb (electric)	nu'ra
brigade	cha'teeva	bun (sweet)	lach'man-ee'ya m'tuka
bright	ba'heer	bundle	cha'vee'la
bring (v.)	l'havee	bureau (office)	mis'rad
broad	ra'chav	burglar	po'rets
broadcast	shi'dur	bus	oto'bus
broil (v.)	litz'lot	business	mis'char
broker	so'chen	busy	a'suk
brooch	see'ka	but	a'val
brook	na'chal	butcher	ka'tsav
broom	ma'ta'tai	butter	chem'a
brother	ach	butterfly	parpar
brotherhood	ach'ava	button	kaf'tor
brother-in-law	guees	buy (v.)	lik'not
brow	me'tsach	buyer	ko'ne
brown	chum		

C

cab	mo'neet	candle	ner
cabbage	k'ruv	candy	su'karee'ya
cabbie	na'hag	cane	ma'kail
cabinet	a'ron	cannon	to'tach
(furniture)		canteen	mai'mee'ya
cablegram	miv'rak	cantor	cha'zan
cactus	tsa'bar	cap (for head)	ko'va
cafe	bait ka'fe	cape (attire)	shich'mi'ya
cage	k'luv	capital (city)	eer-ha'beera
cake	u'ga	capital (wealth)	r'chush
calamity	a'son	capsule	k'mu'sa
calculate (v.)	l'cha'shev	captain (at sea)	rav-cho'vel
calendar	lu'ach	captain (army)	se'ren
calf	e'guel	car	m'cho'neet
calisthenics	hit'am'lut	care	d'a'ga
call (v.)	lik'ro	take care!	hi'za'her!
callus	ya'be'let	careful	za'heer
calm	sha'ket	cargo	mit'an
camel	ga'mal	carnation	tsi'po'ren
camera	mats'le'ma	carp (fish)	karp'yon
camp	ma'cha'ne	carpenter	na'gar
campaign	miv'tsa	carpet	mar'vad
can	kuf'sa	carrot	gue'zer
canal	t'a'la	carry (v.)	lin'so
cancel (v.)	l'va'tel	cart	a'gala
candid	galu'ee-lev	cash	m'zu'man
candidate	mo'o'mad	cashier	ku'pa'ee

7

cat	cha'tul	cheap	zol
catch (v.)	lit'fos	cheat	ra'ma'ee
cattle	ba'kar	check	
cauliflower	k'ru'veet	(restaurant	cheshbon
cave	m'ar'a	bill)	
cease (v.)	lach'dol	check	ham'cha'a
cedar	e'rez	(remittance)	
ceiling	tik'ra	check (v.)	liv'dok
celebration	m'siba;	cheek	le'chee
	cha'gueega	cheerful	a'leez
celery	karpas	cheese	g'vina
cement	me'let	cherry	duv'd'van
cemetery	bait k'va'rot	chess	shach'mat
census	mif'kad	chest	cha'ze
center	mer'kaz	(physical)	
century	me'a	chest	ar'gaz; taiva
cereal	da'gan	(furniture)	
ceremony	te'kes	chew (v.)	lil'os
certain	ba'tu'ach	chicken	tar'n'gol
certainly!	b'va'deye!	chief	rosh
certificate	t'u'da	child	ye'led
chain	shal'shelet	chilly	ka'reer
chair	ki'sai	chimney	a'ruba
chairman	yo'shev rosh	chin	san'ter
chalk	gueer	china	char'see'na
chambermaid	chad'ra'neet	China	seen
champion	a'luf	choice	b'cheera
change (v.)	l'sha'not	choir	mak'he'la
chapter	pe'rek	choke (v.)	lacha'nok
character	o'fee	christen (v.)	l'hatbeel
charity	tsi'daka	Christian	nots'ree
charm	chain	church	k'nesi'ya

8

cinema   **company (business)**

cinema	kol'no'a	coat	m'eel
circle	ma'gal	coiffure	tisro'ket
circumcision	b'rit mee'la	coin	mat'bai'a
citizen	ez'rach	cold	kar
citron	et'rog	cold (ailment)	tsina; na'zelet
city	eer	collar	tsa'va'ron
claim (v.)	lit'bo'a	colleague	a'meet
class (school)	ki'ta	collect (v.)	le'esof
class	sug; ma'amad;	college	michla'la
(position)	dar'ga	color	tse'va
clean (adj.)	na'kee	column	tur
clear	ba'heer	(in publi-	
clerk	pa'keed	cation)	
clever	pikai'ach	column	a'mud
climate	a'kleem	(in building)	
climax	see	comb	mas'rek
climb (v.)	l'ta'pes	combination	tse'ruf
clinic	mir'pa'a	come (v.)	la'vo
clock	sha'on	comfort (v.)	lena'chem
close (v.)	lis'gor	comfortable	no'ach
close (near)	ka'rov	command	p'kuda
closet	a'ron b'gadeem	commander	m'fa'ked
cloth	a'reeg	commemo-	l'hazkeer
clothes	b'gadeem	rate (v.)	
cloud	a'nan	commission	va'a'da
clown	laitzan,	committee	va'ad
	bad'chan	commotion	m'huma
club (enter-	mo'a'don	communicate	l'ho'dee'a
tainment		(v.)	
center)		community	k'hila; aida
coarse	gas	company	chevra
coast	chof	(business)	

9

company (visitors)   **corn (on foot)**

company (visitors)	or'cheem	conservative	shamran (n.); sham'ranee (adj.)
compare (v.)	l'hash'vot		
compass	mats'pen	conspicuous	bo'let
compassion	rachma'nut; chem'la	constant	t'meedee
		constipation	ats'irut
compete (v.)	l'hitcha'rot	consumer	tsar'chan
complaint	t'luna	contented	m'ru'tse
complete	sha'lem	contest	ma'avak; hit'cha'rut
compliment	ma'cha'ma'a		
composer	malcheen	contract	cho'ze
compromise	p'shara	contractor	kab'lan
concen- trate (v.)	l'hit'ra'kez	contribution	t'ruma
		control (v.)	li'shlot
concert	kon'tsert	controversy	sich'such
concrete	be'ton	conversation	see'cha
condition	ma'tsav	convert (to Judaism)	guer (m.), g'yoret (f.)
conductor (orchestra)	m'na'tsai'ach		
		convert (from Judaism)	m'shumad
conductor (train)	kartee'san		
		cook (v.)	l'va'shel
conference	v'eeda; a'saifa	cook	ta'bach
confidence	ai'mun	cookie	u'gui'ya
congestion	ts'fee'fut	cooperate (v.)	l'hish'ta'tef
congratu- lations	ai'chuleem	cop	sho'ter
		copper	n'cho'shet
connection	ke'sher	copy	o'tek
conscience	mats'pun	cord	chevel dak
conscription	guee'yus	cordial	a'deev
consecration	hak'da'sha	cork	p'kak
consecutive	ra'tsuf	corn (edible)	tee'ras
		corn (on foot)	ya'belet

corner	pi'na	criminal	po'shai'a
correct	na'chon	crimson	sha'nee
correct (v.)	l'ta'ken	cripple	na'che
corridor	proz'dor	crisis	mash'ber
cosmetic	tamruk	critic	meva'ker
cost (price)	m'cheer	crocheting	s'reega
costly	ya'kar	crocodile	ta'neen
cotton	kut'na	crook	ga'nav
couch	sa'pa	crooked	a'kum
cough (v.)	l'hish'ta'el	crossroad	tso'met
cough	she'ul	crossword	cheedat
count (v.)	lis'por	puzzle	tash'bets
counterfeit	zi'yuf	crowd	ha'mon
country	erets; medina	crown	ke'ter
couple	zug	crucifix	tslav
court (ball	migrash	cruel	ach'za'ree
playing)		crumbs	peru'reem
court (judicial)	bait mishpat	crust	k'rum
cousin	do'dan (m.);	cry (v.)	liv'kot
	ben	cucumber	mela'fefon
	mish'pacha	cuff	shar'vu'leet
cow	pa'ra	cult	pul'chan
cradle	a'reesa	culture	tar'but
craftsman	u'man	cup	se'fel
crazy	meshu'ga	cure (v.)	l'ra'pe
cream	sha'me'net	cure	ri'pu'ee
whipped		curiosity	sak'ra'nut
cream	katse'fet	curl	tal'tal
credit	ash'reye	currant	dam'd'maneet
(financial)		currency	mat'bai'a
crew	tsevet	foreign	
crime	pe'sha	currency	mat'bai'a zar

curse   **Cyprus**

curse	k'lala	customs	me'ches
curtain	vee'lon	cute	nech'mad
cushion	kar	cutlery	sa'kum
custom	min'hag		(acronym)
customary	ra'gueel	cypress	b'rosh
customer	la'ko'ach	Cyprus	kafri'sin

D

dad	abba
daily	yom-yom
dairy (foods)	chala'vee
damage	ne'zek
damn!	la'a'zazel!
damp	lach
dance (v.)	lir'kod
dance	rikud
danger	sa'ka'na
dark	a'fel
darling	ya'kee'ree (m.), ya'kee'ra'tee (f.)
date (calendar)	ta'areech
date (appoint-ment)	p'gueesha
date (fruit)	ta'mar
daughter	bat
daughter-in-law	ka'la
dawn	sha'char
day	yom
day after tomorrow	mo'cho'ra'ta'yeem
day before yesterday	shil'shom
dead	met (m.)
deaf	che'resh
dear	ya'kar
death	ma'vet
debt	cho'va
Decalogue	a'seret ha-dib'rot
deceive (v.)	l'ra'mot
declaration	hats'ha'ra
decrease	yereeda
deed	ma'a'se
deep	a'mok
deer	tsvee, a'yal
defeat	ma'pa'la
defect	mum, p'gam
defense	ha'gana
deficit	gai'ra'on
definition	hag'da'ra
degree	mad'rai'ga
degree (academic)	to'ar
degree (on measuring device)	ma'ala
delay (v.)	l'hit'ma'mai'ha
delegate	na'tseeg
delete (v.)	lim'chok
delicacy	ma'adan

delicate   **director (stage, film)**

delicate	a'deen	development	hit'pat'chut
delicious	ta'eem	development	shi'kun
delight	o'neg	(housing)	
deluge	ma'bul	devout	da'tee
deluxe	m'hudar	dew	tal
demand (v.)	lid'rosh	diabetes	su'keret
deny (v.)	l'hak'chesh	diagnosis	iv'chun
dentist	ro'fe	dial (v.)	l'cha'yeg
	shi'neye'eem	dialogue	du'see'ach
depart (v.)	l'his'ta'lek	diamond	ya'ha'lom
department	mach'la'ka	diaper	chi'tul
department	cha'nut kol-bo	diarrhea	shilshul
store		diary	yo'man
depot	ta'cha'na	dictator	ro'dan
derogatory	m'zal'zel	dictionary	mi'lon
descend (v.)	la're'det	difference	hev'del
description	te'ur	different	sho'ne
desert	mid'bar	difficult	ka'she
desirable	ra'tsu'ee	digestion	i'kul
desire	t'shu'ka	dignity	ha'dar;
desk	mich'ta'va		ats'eelut
despair	ye'ush	diligence	cha'ree'tsut
despite	lam'rot	dim	kai'he
dessert	ma'na	dimple	gu'mat chen
	acha'ro'na	dine (v.)	lis'od
destiny	go'ral	dining room	cha'dar o'chel
destitute	ev'yon	dinner	s'uda i'ka'reet
destroy (v.)	l'hashmeed	direct (v.)	l'had'reech
detail	p'rat	direct	ya'sheer
detain (v.)	l'a'kev	direction	ki'vun
detective	ba'lash	director	ba'ma'ee
detest (v.)	lis'no	(stage, film)	

14

directory	mad'reech	dossier	teek
dirt	lich'luch	dot	n'kuda
dirty	m'luch'lach	double (v.)	l'hach'peel
disappointment	ach'za'va	double	pee ke'fel
discipline	mish'ma'at	doubt	sa'fek
discount	ha'na'cha	dough	ba'tsek
discovery	guilu'ee	down	l'ma'ta
disease	ma'cha'la	dowry	n'dun'ya
disgrace	cher'pa	doze	nim'num
disgusting	ma'gueel	dozen	t'rai'sar
dish	tsa'la'chat	drawer	m'gai'ra
dispute	sich'such;	dream	cha'lom
	mach'lo'ket	drench (v.)	l'harteev
distance	mer'chak	dress	sim'la
distant	ra'chok	dress (v.)	l'hit'la'besh
distribution	ha'fa'tsa;	(oneself)	
	cha'lu'ka	dressing	ro'tev
district	ma'choze; e'zor	(for food)	
disturb (v.)	l'haf'ree'a	drink (v.)	lish'tot
diver	tso'lel	drink	sh'teeya
divide (v.)	l'cha'lek	drive (v.)	lin'hog
divorce	guet	(vehicle)	
divorced man	ga'rush	driver	ne'hag
divorcee	g'rusha	drizzle	tif'tuf
dizzy	s'char'char	drop	ti'pa
dock	na'mal	dropout	no'sher
doctor	ro'fe	drown (v.)	lit'bo'a
document	mis'mach	drug	r'fu'a; sam
dog	ke'lev	druggist	ro'kai'ach
donation	n'dava	drug store	bait mir'ka'chat
donkey	cha'mor	drum	tof
door	de'let	drunkard	shi'kor

15

dry   **dwelling**

dry	ya'vesh	Dutchman	ho'lan'dee
dry cleaning	ni'ku'ee ya'vesh	Dutch treat	ki'bud kol echad l'ats'mo
duck	bar'vaz	duty-free	pa'tur mi'me'ches
dues	d'mai cha'ver	dwarf	ga'mad
dusk	bain ha'sh'mashot	dwelling	ba'yeet, dee'ra
dust	a'vak		

E

each	kol echad	elastic	ga'meesh
eagle	ne'sher	elbow	mar'pek
ear(s)	o'zen;	elderly	ka'sheesh
	oz'neye'yeem	elect (v.)	liv'chor
earache	k'ev o'zen	elections	b'chee'rot
early	muk'dam	electricity	chash'mal
earring	a'gueel	electrician	chash'ma'leye
earth	a'dama	elegant	m'hu'dar
earthenware	k'lai cho'mer	elementary	b'see'see
east	miz'rach	elevation	ra'ma
Easter	pas'cha	elevator	ma'aleet
easy	kal	eleven	ach'ad-a'sar
eat (v.)	le'ech'ol	embarrass-	m'vu'cha
economy	kal'ka'la	ment	
edition	ma'ha'dura	embassy	shagree'rut
education	chi'nuch	emigrant	m'ha'guer
efficient	ya'eel	emotion	ri'gush
effort	ma'a'mats	emphasis	had'ga'sha
egg	bai'tsa	empty	raik
omelette	cha'veeta	end	sof
scrambled	bai'tsa t'rufa	end (v.)	lig'mor
egg		endorsement	i'shur
eggplant	cha'tseel	enema	cho'ken
Egypt	mits'ra'yeem	enemy	o'yev
eight	sh'mo'ne	energy	me'rets
eighteen	sh'mo'n a-a'sar	engine	ma'no'a
eighty	sh'mo'neem	engineer	m'han'des

engineering   **exchange**

engineering	han'da'sa	erudite	m'lu'mad
England	an'glee'ya	escalator	mad're'got
English (language)	an'gleet		na'ot
		escape (v.)	liv'ro'ach
engraving	cha'ree'ta	escort	m'la've (m.), m'la'va (f.)
enjoyable	m'ha'ne		
enlarge (v.)	l'hag'deel	esplanade	ta'ye'let
enormous	a'na'kee	essential	i'ka'ree
enough	ma'speek	estate	a'chuza
enrage (v.)	l'har'gueez	estimation	ha'a'racha
en route	ba'de'rech	etc.	v'chu'lai
enter (v.)	l'hi'ka'nes	eternity	ne'tsach
entrance	k'nee'sa	even (adv.)	a'fee'lu
enterprise	mif'al	evening	e'rev
entertain (at home) (v.)	l'a'rai'ach	good evening!	e'rev tov!
entertainer	bad'ran	evening clothes	til'bo'shet e'rev
entertainment	bi'dur	event	m'o'ra
enthusiasm	hit'la'ha'vut	every	kol
entirely	l'gam'rai	everybody	kol echad
entree (at table)	ma'na i'ka'reet	everywhere	b'chol ma'kom
envelope	ma'a'ta'fa	evidence	e'dut
environment	s'vee'va	evil	ri'shut
envy	ki'na	exact	m'du'yak
epidemic	ma'gai'fa	exaggerate (v.)	l'hag'zeem
equal	sha've	examination	b'chee'na, b'dee'ka
equipment	tsee'yud		
erase (v.)	lim'chok	example	dugma
eraser	mo'chek	excellence	hits'ta'yi'nut
errand	sh'lee'chut	except	chuts mee...
error	ta'ut	exchange (v.)	l'ha'cha'leef

excitement   **eyewitness**

excitement	hit'rag'shut	explosive	cho'mer ne'fets
excursion	ti'yul	export	yi'tsu
excuse (v.)	lis'lo'ach	exterior	chee'tsonee
excuse	te'ruts	extra	no'saf
exempt	pa'tur mee...	extraordinary	yo'tsai
exhale (v.)	lin'shof		min'ha'klal
exhibition	ha'tsa'ga	extreme,	keetso'nee
exit	ye'tsee'a	extremist	
expedite (v.)	l'ha'cheesh	eye(s)	a'yeen;
expense	ho'tsa'a;		ai'na'yeem
	tash'lum	eyebrow	ga'ba
expensive	ya'kar	eyeglasses	mishka'fa'yeem
experience	ni'sa'yon	sun glasses	mish'k'fai
expert	mum'che		she'mesh
explain (v.)	l'hasbeer	eyelash	rees
explanation	hes'ber	eyelid	af'af
exploit (v.)	l'na'tsel	eye shadow	ee'pur a'yeen
		eyewitness	ed r'ee'ya

F

fable	ma'shal, a'gada	fashion	of'na
fabric	a'reeg	fashion	
face	pa'neem	show	tsu'gat of'na
fact	uv'da	fast	ma'heer
factory	bait charo'shet	fast (v.)	la'tsum
failure	ki'sha'lon	fast day	yom tsom
faint (v.)	l'hit'a'lef	fat (adj.)	sha'men
fair	m'hu'gan	fat	shu'man
faith	e'mu'na	fate	go'ral
faithful	ne'e'man	father	av
fake (v.)	l'za'yef	forefathers	a'vot
fall (v.)	lin'pol	father-in-law	cho'ten
fall (autumn)	s'tav	fatherland	mo'le'det
fall in love (v.)	l'hit'a'hev	fatigue	a'yai'fut
fame	pir'sum	faulty	pa'gum,
familiar	ya'du'a		m'kulkal
family	mish'pa'cha	fauna	o'lam ha'cheye
famished	go'vai'a	favor	to'va
	mi'ra'av	fear	pa'chad
fan (to create	m'neefa	feast	s'uda
wind)		Feast of	chag
fanatic	ka'na'ee	Weeks	ha'sha'vuot
far	ra'chok	(Shavuot)	
fare (for travel)	d'mai n'see'a	feather	nots
farewell	bir'kat p'reeda	fee	sa'char
farm	me'shek	feeble	cha'lash
farmer	i'kar	feed (v.)	l'ha'acheel

feel (v.)   **flat**

feel (v.)	l'hargueesh	finger nail	tsi'po'ren
feeling	har'gasha	fingernail	mish'chat
fellow	bar'nash; a'dam	polish	tsi'por'neye'-
female	n'kaiva		im
fence	ga'der	fir	a'shu'ach
fertile	po're	fire	esh; d'laika
festival	chag	fire alarm	a'zakat s'raifa
festive	cha'guee'guee	fire brigade	m'cha'bai esh
fever	ka'da'chat;	fireman	ka'ba'ee
	chom	first	ri'shon
few	a'cha'deem	first aid	ezra ri'shona
fiance (e)	a'rus, a'rusa	first born	b'chor (m.),
field	sa'de		b'chora (f.)
fifteen	chamesh-esrai	first class	mad're'ga
fifty	cha'meesheem		rish'ona
fig	t'en'na	first cousin	do'dan ri'shon
fight	k'rav, ma'avak	first name	shem p'ra'tee
figure (form)	tsu'ra	fish	dag
figure (mathe-	mis'par	fish (v.)	la'dug
matics)		fisherman	da'yag
filling station	ta'chanat de'lek	fist	e'grof
film	se'ret	five	cha'mesh
filth	lichluch	five hundred	cha'mesh me'ot
financial	kas'pee	fix (v.)	l'ta'ken
find (v.)	lim'tso	fix (a time) (v.)	l'sa'der, likbo'a
find	m'tsee'a	flag	de'guel
(a bargain)		flame	shal'he'vet
fine (adj.)	a'deen, na'e,	flamingo	sh'kee'tan
	m'shu'bach	flashlight	pa'nas kees
fine	k'nas	flashlight	sole'lat-
(punishment)		battery	mav'zek
finger	ets'ba	flat (adj.)	cha'lak

flat (apartment)   **free**

flat (apartment)	dee'ra
flavor	ta'am m' yuchad
flesh	ba'sar
flesh and blood	ba'sar v'dam
flight	tee'sa
floor	rits'pa
floor (storey)	ko'ma
flora	o'lam hatso'mai'ach
flour	ke'mach
flow (v.)	liz'rom
flower	pe'rach
flower shop	cha'nut p'racheem
flu	sha'pa'at
flute	cha'leel
fly (v.)	la'tus
fly	z'vuv
fog	a'ra'fel
fold (v.)	l'ka'pel
folder	ot'fan
folk song	sheer-am
folksy	a'mamee
food	o'chel, ma'zon
fool	ti'pesh
foot; feet	re'guel; rag'leye'eem
forecast (weather)	ta'cha'zeet
foreign	zar
foreign minister	sar ha'chuts
forest	ya'ar
forever	l'o'lam
forget (v.)	lish'ko'ach
forgiveness	s'leecha
fork	maz'leg
fort	miv'tsar
fortnight	sh'vu-eye-eem
fortunate	bar-ma'zal
fortune	hon
forty	ar'ba'eem
forward!	ka'dee'ma!
foster family	mish'pacha o'menet
foundation	y'sod
fountain	ma'yan
fountain pen	et no've'a
four	ar'ba
fourteen	arba-es'rai
fowl	of
fox	shu'al
foyer	p'rozdor
fracture	she'ver
fragrant	ba'sum
frame	mis'gueret
France	tsor'fat
frank	g'lu'ee-lev
frankfurter	nak'nee'keet
freckle	ne'mesh
free	chof'shee; panu'ee

free (of cost)   **future**

free (of cost)	l'lo tash'lum; chee'nam	fruit(s)	p'ree, pe'rot
freedom	cho'fesh, che'rut	fruit juice	meets pe'rot
freeze (v.)	l'hak'pee	fruit salad	sa'lat pe'rot
freezer	mak'pee	fry pan	ma'cha'vat
French fries	tchi'peem	fuel	de'lek
frequent	ta'deer	full	ma'lai
fresh (food, air)	ta'ree, ra'an'an	fund	ke'ren
		fundamental	ye'sodee
fresh (insolent)	chuts'pa'nee	funeral	leva'ya
Friday	yom shi'shee	fur	par'va
fried	m'tu'gan	furnish (v.)	l'sa'pek; l'tsa'yed
friend	ye'deed; cha'ver	furniture	ra'heet'eem
frog	ts'far'dai'a	fury	za'am
from	min	fuse	na'teech
frontier	g'vul	fuss	es'ek rav
frugal	chas'cha'nee	future	a'teed

23

G

gale	su'fa	gender	meen
gall bladder	kees ha'mara	genealogy	to'la'dot; se'der yichu'seen
gallows	gar'dom		
galoshes	ar'daleem	general (adj.)	k'lalee
gambling	hi'mur	general (military)	a'luf
game	mis'chak		
gang	k'nu'fee'ya	generation	dor
garage	mu'sach	generous	na'deev
garbage	ze'vel, ash'pa	genius	ga'on
garden	gan, guee'na	gentile	lo yehudee; goy
gargle (v.)	l'gar'guer	gentle	a'deen
garland	zer	gentleman	ben-tar'but
garlic	shum	genuine	a'mee'tee
garment	mal'bush	germ	cheye'dak
garrulous	m'fat'pet	ghoul	ru'ach ra'a; shed
garter	bee'reet		
gasoline	ben'zeen	giant	a'nak
gas pump	mash'ai'vat ben'zeen	gift	ma'ta'na
		ginger	zan'g'vil
gate	sha'ar	girdle	cha'go'ra
gather (v.)	le'e'sof	girl; (teen-age girl)	yal'da; (na'ara)
gathering	a'sai'fa; ke'nes		
gaze (v.)	l'his'ta'kel	girlfriend	ba'chu'ra, yedeeda
gaze	ma'bat		
gear (in vehicle)	hi'luch	gist	tam'tseet
		give (v.)	la'tet
gem	e'ven tova	gladiola	se'fen

glass		grace	chen, che'sed
(drinking)	kos	grace (after	bir'kat
glass	z'chu'cheet	meal)	ha'mazon
glazier	za'gag	graduate	bo'guer
gleam	ni'tsuts	(college)	
glee	gueel	graduation	te'kes
gloomy	a'fel, a'tsuv	(lower	ha'si'yum
glorious	m'fo'ar,	grades)	
	ne'he'dar	grammar	dik'duk
glory	hod	granary	go'ren
glove	k'faya, k'saya	grandson,	neched,
glue	de'vek	grand-	nech'da
gnat	ya'tush	daughter	
go (v.)	la'lechet	grandfather	sav
goal	ma'ta'ra	grandma	sav'ta
goat	ta'yeesh	grandmother	sa'va
God	HaShem;	grandpa	sa'ba
	Elo'heem	grand total	sach ha'kol
godfather	san'dak	granite	sha'cham
goiter	za'pe'ket	grape	e'nav
gold	za'hav	grapefruit	esh'ko'leet
goldfish	z'hav'nun, dag	grapefruit	mits esh'ko'
	za'hav	juice	lee'yot
good	tov	grass	e'sev, de'she
good-hearted	tov-lev	grasshopper	cha'gav
good morning	bo'ker tov	gratuity	ma'tat
good night	leye'la tov	grave (tomb)	ke'ver
gossip	r'cheelut	gravestone	ma'tse'va
gout	tseen'eet	gray	a'for
government	mem'shala	Greece	ya'van
governor	mo'shel	green	ya'rok
gown	sim'la	greengrocer	yar'kan
		vegetables	y'ra'kot

25

greeting   **gypsy**

greeting	b'racha	guard	sho'mer
grenade	ri'mon	guest	o'rai'ach
griddlecake	l'veeva	guide	mad'reech
grief	ya'gon	guilty	a'shem
grievance	t'lu'na	gum (chewing)	mas'teek
grippe	sha'pa'at	gums (dental)	cha'neech'-
grocery	ma'ko'let		a'yeem
ground	kar'ka	gun	ek'dach
group	k'vutsa	gym	u'lam hit'am'lut
grow (v.)	li'g'dol; l'ga'del	gypsy	tso'a'nee

H

habit	her'guel
hail	ba'rad
hair	se'ar
hairbrush	mis'eret
haircut	tis'po'ret
hairdresser	sa'par
hair style	tis'ro'ket
half	cha'tsee
hall	u'lam
hallow (v.)	l'ka'desh
hamlet	k'far ka'tan
hammer	pa'teesh
hammock	ar'sal
hand(s)	yad, ya'da'yeem
handbag	teek
handball	ka'dur yad
handkerchief	mim'cha'ta
handle	ya'deet
handmade	a'vodat yad
handsome	na'e, ya'fe (m.)
hanger	ko'lav
happening	mik're
happiness	sim'cha, o'sher
hard	ka'she
hardship	m'tsu'ka
hardware	k'lai ma'te'chet
harm	ne'zek

harp	ne'vel
harvest	ka'tseer
hassock	ka'reet
hat	ko'va
hatred	si'na
haven	mik'lat
hawk	nets
hazardous	m'su'kan
he	hu
head	rosh
headache	k'ev rosh
headlight	pa'nas kidmee
headline	ko'teret
heal (v.)	l'ra'pai
health	b'ree'ut
to your health!	la'b'ri'ut!
healthy	ba'ree (m.), b'ree'a (f.)
healthful	mav'ree
hear (v.)	lish'mo'a
heart	lev
heartache	k'ev lev
heart attack	het'kef lev
heartburn	tsa're'vet
heat	chom
heat (v.)	l'cha'mem

27

heat wave   **hotplate**

heat wave	gal chom	hire (v.)	li'skor
heaven	sha'ma'yeem;	hit (v.)	lif'go'a; l'ha'kot
	gan e'den	hitchhiker	trem'pist
heavy	ka'ved	honest	ya'shar
Hebrew	iv'reet	honey	d'vash
(language)		honeymoon	yerach d'vash
heel	a'kev	honor	ka'vod
height	go'va	hoodlum	bir'yon
heir	yo'resh	hook	vav
helicopter	ma'sok	hope	tik'va
hell	gai'hi'nom	horizon	o'fek
help	ez'ra	horn	ke'ren
help! (in	ha'tsee'lu!	ram's horn	sho'far
emergency)		horrible	ma'cha'reed
help (v.)	la'azor	horse	sus
hen	tarn'go'let	horseradish	cha'zeret
here	kan	horticulture	gana'nut
heretic	a'pi'ko'res	hose (wear-	guerev,
heritage	ye'rush'a	able)	puz'mak
hero(ine)	guee'bor (m),	hose (for	tsi'nor gumee
	guee'bora (f.)	watering)	
herring	dag ma'lu'ach	hospital	bait cho'leem
hesitate (v.)	l'ha'ses	hospitality	hach'nasat
hiccup (v.)	l'sha'hek		or'cheem
high	ga'vo'ha	host	m'a'rai'ach
highbrow	mas'keel	hostel	ach'san'ya
high school	bait-sefer	hot	cham
	tee'chon	hot (condi-	cha'reef
highway	k'vish ro'shee	ments)	
hill	guee'va; tel	hot dog	nak'nee'keet
hint	re'mez	hotel	ma'lon
hip	ya'rech	hotplate	tsa'la'chat
			bi'shul

28

hot water   **hypocrisy**

hot water	ma'yeem cha'meem	hunger	ra'av
hot water bottle	bak'buk cham	hungry	ra'ev
hour	sha'a	hunter	tsa'yad
house	ba'yeet	hurray!	hai'dad!
housewarming	chanu'kat ha'ba'yeet	hurry	chi'pa'zon
		hurt	p'guee'a
how	aich	husband	ba'al
hug (v.)	l'cha'bek	husk	k'lipa
hum (v.)	l'zam'zem	hut	su'ka; ts'reef
human	e'nushee		
humane	rach'ma'nee	hyacinth	ya'keen'ton
humble	a'nav; tsa'nu'a	hydrant	zar'nuk
humid	lach	hyena	tsa'vo'a
humor	b'dee'chut	hygiene	gue'hut
hunchback	gui'ben	hymn	sheer ha'lel
hundred	me'a	hyperbole	guz'ma
two hundred	ma'ta'yeem	hypocrisy	tsvee'ut

29

I

I	a'nee	imitation	chi'ku'ee
ibex	ya'el	immediately	mi'yad
ice	ke'rach	immoral	bil'tee
ice cream	g'leeda		mu'sa'ree
ice water	mai-ke'rach	immortal	nits'chee
idea	ra'yon	impatient	lo sav'lan
ideal	mo'fet	implement (v.)	l'hag'sheem
identical	do'me	import	y'vu
identity	ze'hut	important	cha'shuv
idiom	neev	impossible	ee-ef'shar
idle	ba'tel	impression	ro'shem
idler	ats'lan	imprisonment	ma'asar
idol	e'leel	improve (v.)	l'sha'per
if	im; u'leye	improvement	shi'pur
ignite (v.)	l'hatseet	inaccurate	lo nach'on,
ignition	ha'tsata		lo m'du'yak
ignoramus	bur	inactive	lo pa'eel
ill	cho'le (m.),	inadequate	lo mas'peek
	cho'la (f.)	inane	sh'tutee
illegal	lo chu'kee	inappropriate	lo mat'eem
illiterate	an'alfa'be'tee	inception	hat'cha'la
ill-mannered	lo m'nu'mas	inclusive	ko'lel
illness	ma'cha'la	income tax	mas hach'na'sa
illuminate (v.)	l'hav'heer	incompetent	lo m'su'gal
illusion	ash'la'ya	incomplete	lo sha'lem
image	d'mut	incompre-	lo mu'van
imagination	dim'yon	hensible	

30

inconvenient
intellect

inconvenient	lo no'ach	inhale (v.)	lin'shof
incorrect	lo na'chon	initiative	yoz'ma
independent	ats'ma'ee	injection	z'ree'ka
independence	ats'ma'ut	injury	pe'tsa
index	maf'te'ach	injustice	ee'tse'dek
India	ho'du	ink	d'yo
indifferent	a'deesh	inn	pun'dak
indigestion	kilkul kai'va	inner	p'neemee
individual	ya'cheed	innovation	chi'dush
indoors	ba'ba'yeet	inquiry	cha'keera
industrialist	ta'asee'yan	inquisitive	sak'ra'nee
industrious	cha'ruts	insane	lo sha'fu'ee;
inedible	lo a'cheel		m'to'raf
inexcusable	she'lo yi'sa'lach	insect	cha'rak
inexpensive	zol	inside	p'nee'ma
infantile	yal'du'tee	insight	to'va'na
infantryman	cha'yal rag'lee	insignia	i'tu'reem
inferior	na'chut	inspiring	mal'heev
infirm	cha'lush	instance	dug'ma
infirmary	mir'pa'a	instant	re'gua
inflammation	da'leket	instantaneous	mi'ya'dee
inflation	ni'pu'ach	instead	bim'kom
influence	hash'pa'a	institute	ma'chon
influenza	sha'pa'at	institution	mo'sad
inform (v.)	l'ho'dee'a	instruction	li'mud, ho'ra'a,
informal	lo rish'mee		had'ra'cha
information	mai'da	instructor	mad'reech
ingenious	m'chu'kam	instrument	mach'sheer
ingenuous	ta'meem,	insult	el'bon
	ya'shar	insult (v.)	l'ha'aleev
ingredient	mar'keev	insurance	bi'tu'ach
inhabitant	to'shav	intellect	bee'na, se'chel

31

intelligence bureau   **ivy**

intelligence bureau	a'gaf mo'dee'een	introduction (in a book)	ma'vo
intelligent	na'von	invader	po'lesh
intention	ka'va'na	invention	ham'tsa'a
interest	in'yan	invest (v.)	l'hash'kee'a
interest (bank, bond)	ri'beet	investigation	cha'kee'ra
		investment	hash'ka'a
interest (v.)	l'an'yen	invitation	haz'ma'na
interesting	m'any'yen	ire	ka'as
interfere (v.)	l'hit'a'rev	iron (metal)	bar'zel
interment	k'vu'ra	iron (for pressing)	mag'hets
international	bain l'u'mee	iron (v.)	l'ga'hets
interpret (v.)	l'fa'resh	irregular	lo sa'deer
interruption	haf'ra'a	irrigate (v.)	l'hash'kot
interview	r'a'yon	island	ee
intestine	m'ee	isolation	bi'dud
intricate	m'su'bach	Italian	ee'tal'kee
introduce (v.)	l'hatseeg	itch	gai'ru'ee
introduction (personal)	ha'tsa'ga	ivy	kee'sos

J

jackal	tan	Jewish	ye'hu'dee
jackass	cha'mor; sho'te	Jewry	ya'ha'dut
jacket	m'eel	job	mis'ra
jackknife	o'lar	jobless	muv'tal
jail	ma'asar; ke'le	join (v.)	l'hits'ta'ref
jam (edible)	ree'ba	Jordan	yar'den
janitor	sho'er	journal (diary)	yo'man
jar	tsin'tse'net	journalist	i'to'na'ee
jaundice	tsa'he'vet	journey	ma'sa, n'see'a
jaw	le'set	joy	sim'cha
jealous	m'ka'ne	jubilee	yo'vel
Jerusalem	y'ru'sha'la'yeem	Judaism	ya'ha'dut
jest	b'dee'cha	judge	sho'fet
Jesus	ye'shu ha'notsree	judge (v.)	lish'pot, la'dun
jet (plane)	si'lon	jug	kad
Jew (m.) (f.)	ye'hu'dee, ye'hu'dee'ya	juice	mits
		juicy	a'see'see
jewel	e'ven to'va	jump	k'fee'tsa
jeweler	tso'ref	junk	g'ru'ta'ot
jewelry	tach'shee'teem	juror	mush'ba
		justice	tse'dek

K

keep	l'ha'cha'zeek	kiss	n'shee'ka
keepsake	maz'ke'ret	kiss (v.)	l'na'shek
kernel	gar'een	kitchen	mit'bach
ketchup	tav'leen	kitten	cha'tal'tul
	ag'va'nee'yot	knapsack	tarmeel gav
kettle	kumkum	knee	be'rech
key	maf'tai'ach	kneel (v.)	li'ch'ro'a
kick (v.)	liv'ot	knicknack	tach'sheet
kidney	kli'ya	knife	sa'keen
kidney bean	shu'eet	knit (v.)	lis'rog
kill (v.)	la'ha'rog	knitting	s'ree'ga
kind (adj.)	tov lev	knock	d'fee'ka
kindergarten	gan y'ladeem	knot	ke'sher
kindle	l'hadleek	know (v.)	la'da'at
king	me'lech	knowledge	y'dee'a; ye'da
kinsman	k'rov dam	knuckle	pe'rek ets'ba
		kosher	ka'sher

L

label	ta'veet	landlady	ba'a'lat ha'ba'yeet
labor	a'voda; a'mal	landlord	ba'al ha'ba'yeet
laboratory	ma'a'bada	landscape	nof
laborer	po'el	lane	sh'veel
lace	tach'reem	language	la'shon, sa'fa
lace (for shoes)	s'roch	lantern	pa'nas
lack	cho'ser	lap	chaik
lacking	b'lee, cha'ser	lapel	dash ha'be'gued
lad	tsa'eer, ba'chur	large	ga'dol
ladder	su'lam	laryngitis	da'le'ket ha'ga'ron
laden	a'mus		
ladies room	she'ru'teem li'g'va'rot	lass	ba'chu'ra, na'a'ra
ladle	ma'tse'ket	last	a'cha'ron
lady	g'veret	last name	shem mish'pa'cha
lake	a'gam		
lamb	ke'ves	last night	e'mesh
lamb chop	tse'la ke'ves	late	m'u'char
lame	chi'guer	lather	ke'tsef
lamentation	mis'ped	latrine	bait ki'sai
lamp	me'no'ra; nu'ra	laugh (v.)	li'ts'chok
lampshade	so'chech	laughter	ts'chok
lance	ro'mach	laundry	k'vee'sa
land	ya'ba'sha, a'da'ma	law	chok, mish'pat
land (v.)	lin'chot	lawful	chu'kee
landing	n'chee'ta	lawn	mid'sha'a

35

lawyer

lever

lawyer	o'rech deen	left (direction)	s'mol
laxative	m'shal'shel	left-handed	s'mo'lee
lay (v.)	l'ha'nee'ach	leftovers (at	shi'ra'yeem
layer	shich'va	table)	
layer cake	u'gat r'va'deem	leg	re'guel
layette	tsor'chai tee'nok	legacy	y'ru'sha
lazy	a'tsel	legal	chu'kee
lead (v.)	lin'hog	legend	a'ga'da
lead	o'fe'ret	legible	ka'ree
leader	man'heeg	legislature	bait m'cho'ki'-keem
leaf	a'le		
leaflet	a'lon	leisure	p'neye
leak	d'lee'fa	leisurely	bim'tee'nut
lean	ra'ze	lemon	li'mon
leap	k'fee'tsa	lend (v.)	l'ha'sheel
leap year	shana m'u'be'ret	lend (money)	l'hal'vot
learn (v.)	lil'mod	(v.)	
learn by		length	o'rech
heart	lil'mod al peh	lenient	rach
learner	lo'med (m.),	lens	a'da'sha
	lo'me'det (f.)	leopard	na'mer
leash	r'tsu'a	less	pa'chot
least	pa'chot b'yo'ter	lesson	she'ur
leather	or	letter	ot
leave (depart)	la'a'zov	(alphabet)	
(v.)		letter	mich'tav
leave (over)	l'ha'sheer	letter carrier	da'var
(v.)		letter of credit	mich'tav
lecture	har'tsa'a		ash'reye
lecture (scold)	l'ha'teef	lettuce	cha'sa
(v.)		level	go'va
ledger	se'fer	lever	ma'nof
	chesh'bo'not		

levy	mas	linen	pish'tan
lewdness	zee'na	lingerie	l'va'neem
liar	shak'ran	lining	bit'na
liberate (v.)	l'shach'rer	lint	mir'pad
liberty	cho'fesh, che'rut	lion	ar'ye
librarian	saf'ran	lip(s)	sa'fa,
library	sif'ri'ya		s'fa'ta'yeem
license	rish'yon	lipstick	s'fa'ton
lick (v.)	lil'kok	liquid	no'zel
lie (deceive) (v.)	l'sha'ker	liquor	ma'sh'ke
			cha'reef
lie (down) (v.)	lish'kav	list	r'shee'ma
lie (untruth)	she'ker	listen (v.)	l'hak'sheev,
lieutenant	se'guen		l'ha'a'zeen
lieutenant colonel	s'gan a'luf	literary	sif'ru'tee
		literature	sif'rut
life	cha'yeem	litter (dirt)	ash'pa
lifebelt	cha'gorat	little	ka'tan, pa'ut;
	ha'tsa'la		k'tsat
lifeguard	ma'tseel	little finger (pinky)	ze'ret
life insurance	bi'tu'ach cha'yeem	liturgy	pul'chan
lift (v.)	l'ha'reem	live (v.)	li'ch'yot
light	or	live (adj.)	cheye
light (adj.)	kal; ba'heer	livelihood	par'na'sa
lightning	ba'rak	liver	ka'ved
likable	cha'veev	living quarters	m'gu'reem
like (v.)	l'cha'bev	living room	tra'k'leen
limb	gaf	load	mit'an
limit	ka'tse	loaf (of bread)	ki'kar
linden (tree)	til'ya		
line	shu'ra; kav	loafer	bat'lan

37

loan (money)   **lynx**

loan (money)	hal'va'a	loud	b'kol ram
lobby	mis'de'ron	loudspeaker	ram'kol
local	m'ko'mee	lounge	cha'dar
locale	s'vee'va		or'cheem
lock	man'ul	louse	ki'na
lock (v.)	lin'ol, lach'som	lout	bur
locket	mas'kee'ya	lovable	cha'veev, a'huv
locust	ar'be	love	a'hava
lodge (v.) (in	la'lun,	love (v.)	le'e'hov
inn, hotel)	l'hit'ach'sen	lovely	nech'mad,
logic	hi'ga'yon		ne'he'dar
lone	bo'ded	low	na'moch
lonesome	gal'mud	low gear	hi'luch na'moch
long (adj.)	a'roch	loyal	ne'e'man
long (for) (v.)	l'hit'ga'gai'a	lucid	ba'rur
longevity	a'ree'chut	luck	ma'zal
	ya'meem	good luck!	ma'zal tov!
longshoreman	sa'var	lucrative	mish'ta'lem
look (v.)	l'his'ta'kel,	luggage	miz'va'dot
	l'ha'beet	lullaby	sheer e'res
look	ma'bat	lump	gush
loose	ra'fe, ta'lush,	lunar	y'ra'chee
	chof'shee	lunch	a'ru'chat
loot	sha'lal		tso'ho'reye'-
lord	a'don, a'tseel		eem
lose (v.)	l'a'bed,	lung	rai'a
	l'haf'seed	luscious	ta'eem
loss	a'vai'da	lush	a'see'see
lotion	tar'cheets	lust	ta'va
lottery	hag'ra'la	lynx	cha'tul pe're

M

macaroni	itri'yot	male (adj.)	shel-za'char
machine	m'cho'na	malice	re'sha
mackerel	kol'yas	mallet	ma'ke'vet
mad (adj.)	m'to'raf; ro'guez; m'shu'ga	malodorous	mas'ree'ach
		mama	i'ma
madam	g've'ret	mammal	yo'nek
magazine	k'tav et	man	eesh; guever
magic	ke'sem	management	hanha'la
magnificent	m'fo'ar	mania	shi'ga'on
mahogany	to'la'na	manicure	tishpo'ret
maid	o'zeret; m'sho'retet	mankind	e'nu'shut
		manly	gav'ree
maiden (adj.)	lo n'su'a	manner	o'fen
mail	do'ar	man of means	ba'al emtsa'ut
mailbox	tai'vat mich'ta'veem	manor	a'chu'za
		manpower	ko'ach a'dam
mailman	da'var	mansion	ar'mon
main (adj.)	ro'shee; i'ka'ree	manufacture	y'tsur
maintain (v.)	lit'moch	many	har'be
majestic	mal'chu'tee	map	ma'pa
major (military)	rav-se'ren	maple	e'der
		marble	sha'yeesh
major (adj.)	ba'cheer, ru'ba'nee	march	mits'ad
		marigold	o'guel
majority	rov	marital status	ma'amad ez'ra'chee
make (v.)	la'a'sot; li'tsor	marital	shel-nisu'eem

mark   **men's room**

mark	see'man	maxim	mem'ra
mark (v.)	l'tsa'yen	maybe	u'leye; ef'shar; yi'ta'chen
markdown (pricing)	ha'na'cha	mayor	rosh ha'eer
market	shuk	me	lee; o'tee
marriage	ni'su'eem	meager	dal, ra'ze
married (adj.)	na'su'ee (m.); n'su'a (f.)	meal	a'ru'cha
		mean (adj.)	kam'tsan
marry (v.)	lin'so i'sha; l'hit'cha'ten	mean (v.)	l'hit'ka'ven
		meanwhile	baina'ta'yeem
marsh	bi'tsa	measles	cha'tsevet
marvel	pe'le	measure	mi'da
marvel (v.)	l'hit'pa'el	measure (v.)	lim'dod
marvelous	nif'la	meat	ba'sar
mascara	puch aina'yeem	meat ball	k'tseetsa
mask	ma'se'cha	meat market	it'leez
massacre	te'vach	mechanic	m'cho'na'ee
massage (v.)	lim'shosh	medal	i'tur
masseur (euse)	as'yan(eet)	medicine	r'fu'a; t'ru'fa
mat	mid'ra'sa	mediocre	bai'no'nee
match (matri- monial)	shi'duch	Mediterranean Sea	yam tee'chon
matchmaker	shad'chan	meet (v.)	l'hi'pa'guesh
match (v.)	l'hash'vot, l'ha'teem	meeting	a'saifa
		melt (v.)	lin'mos
match (for fire)	gaf'rur	memorandum	taz'keer
match (contest)	tacha'rut	Memorial Day	yom ha'zi'karon
mate	ben-zug; a'meet	menace	sa'ka'na
material (adj.)	chom'ree	mend (v.)	l'ta'ken, l'sha'pets
material	cho'mer		
mattress	miz'ron	men's room	she'ru'teem l'g'va'reem
mature	m'vu'gar		

menu   **model**

menu	taf'reet	minister (govern-mental)	sar
mercantile	mis'cha'ree		
merchandise	s'cho'ra	minister (diplomatic)	tseer
merchant	so'cher		
merciful	racha'ma'nee	minister (v.)	l'ta'pel
merry	a'leez, sa'me'ach	mink	chor'pan
		minority	m'ut
mess	bil'bul	minus	pa'chot
message	me'ser	minute	da'ka
messenger	sha'lee'ach	miracle	nes
metal	ma'te'chet	mirror	mar'e; r'ee
method	shee'ta	miscalculation	chesh'bon mut'e
mezzanine	ko'mat bai-na'yeem	miscarriage	ha'pa'la
		miscount	ta'ut bis'feera
microbe	cheye'dak	miser	kam'tsan
middle	em'tsa	mishap	ta'ka'la
midnight	cha'tsot	missing (adj.)	ne'edar
midwife	m'ya'le'det	mission	shli'chut
might	ko'ach, ots'ma	mist	ed
mild	ma'tun, na'eem	mistake	ta'ut, sh'guee'a
military (adj.)	tsva'ee	Mister	a'don; mar
milk	cha'lav	mix (v.)	l'ar'bev
mind	mo'ach	mixture	ta'aro'vet
mine (for digging)	mich're	mixup	tis'bo'chet
		moan	a'na'cha
mine (in minefield)	mo'kesh	mob	ha'mon, a'saf'suf
mine (possessive)	she'lee	mobilization	gui'yus
		mock (v.)	l'lagleg
minister (religious)	ko'hen dat	model	tav'neet, deguem

model (fashion)   **motorcycle**

model (fashion)	dug'ma'neet (f.)	mop (v.)	l'na'guev
		mop	mat'leet
moderate (adj.)	ma'tun	moral (adj.)	mu'sa'ree
modern	cha'deesh	morality	mu'sar
modest	tsa'nu'a	morale	mish'ma'at
moist	lach, ra'tov	more	yo'ter, no'saf, od
molasses	div'sha		
moldy	a'vash	morning	bo'ker
molest (v.)	l'hatseek	good	
mollify (v.)	l'fa'yes	morning	bo'ker tov
mollycoddle (v)	l'fa'nek	morning star	a'ye'let ha'sha'char
monastery	min'zar	Moroccan	maro'ka'nee
Monday	yom she'nee	morose	a'gum
money	ke'sef, ma'mon	mortgage	mash'kan'ta
money order	ham'cha'at ke'sef	mosque	mis'gad
		mosquito	ya'tush
monitor	to'ran	most	ha'yoter, ha'chee
monitor (v.)	l'hash'guee'ach		
monk	na'zeer	mostly	al pee rov
monkey	kof	moth	ash
monotonous	chad'go'nee	mother	em
monster	mif'le'tset	mother-in-law (husband's mother)	cha'mot
month	cho'desh		
monthly	chod'shee		
monthly publication	yar'chon	mother-in-law (wife's mother)	cho'te'net
monument	an'dar'ta		
monument (in cemetery)	ma'tse'va	motherland	mo'le'det
		motion	t'nu'a
mood	matsav ru'ach	motor	ma'no'a
moon	l'vana, ya're'ach	motorcycle	of'no'a

42

motor scooter	kat'no'a	mud	bots
mound	tel	mule	pir'da
mount (a	la'a'lot	multiply (v.)	l'hachpeel
horse) (v.)		mumps	cha'ze'ret
mountain	har	municipality	eeree'ya
mourner	a'vel	munitions	tach'mo'shet
mouse	ach'bar	murder	re'tsach
moustache	sa'fam	murderer	ro'tse'ach
mouth	pe	muscle	sh'reer
move (v.)	l'ha'nee'a	mushroom	pitri'ya
movement	t'nu'a	mustard	char'dal
movie (theatre)	kol'no'a	mute	i'lem
movie film	se'ret	mutual	ha'da'dee
much	har'be, m'od	mystery	ta'alu'ma

43

N

nail (fingernail)	tsi'po'ren	needle	ma'chat
		negative	shlee'lee
nail (for hammering)	mas'mer	negotiation	ma'sa u'ma'tan
		neighbor	sha'chen
nail file	ma'shof l'-tsipor'neye'eem	neighborhood	sh'chu'na
		nephew	ach'yan
naive	ta'meem	nerve(s)	a'tsab(eem)
naked	a'rom	nervous	ats'ba'nee
name	shem	nest	ken
nap	t'nu'ma	net	re'shet
napkin	ma'peet	never	l'olam lo; af pa'am
narrow	tsar		
nation	u'ma, l'om	nevertheless	af al pee chen
national	l'u'mee	new	cha'dash
native	y'leed	news	cha'da'shot
natural	tee'vee	newspaper	i'ton
nausea	b'cheela	next	ha'ba
navel	ta'bur	nice	na'e, nech'mad
navigator	na'vat	niece	ach'ya'neet
navy	chail ha'yam	night	leye'la
near	ka'rov	good night	leye'la tov
nearly	kim'at	night club	mo'a'don leye'la
necessity	tso'rech	nine	te'sha
neck	tsa'var	nineteen	t'sha-esrai
necklace	a'nak; ma'cha'ro'zet	ninety	tish'eem
		no	lo
necktie	a'nee'va	noise	ra'ash

none	af lo e'chad; k'lal lo	novel	ro'man
		now	ach'shav; a'ta
noodle	it'riya	number	mis'par
noon	tso'ho'reye'eem	nun	n'zeera
normal	ta'keen	nurse	a'chot rach'- ma'nee'ya
north	tsa'fon		
nose	af, cho'tem	nursery (for children)	cha'dar y'la'deem
nostril	na'cheer		
note	pe'tek	nursery (plants)	mish'ta'la
note (v.)	lir'shom		
notebook	pin'kas		
nothing	e'fes	nut	e'goz
notice	ho'fa'a	nutrition	t'zu'na

O

oaf	sho'te	official (adj.)	rish'mee
oak	a'lon	official	pa'keed
oath	sh'vu'a	often	l'iteem k'ro'vot
oatmeal	ke'mach shi'bolet shu'al	oil	she'men; neft
		ointment	mish'cha
object	che'fets	old (person)	za'ken; ka'sheesh
objective	ma'ta'ra		
obligation	cho'va	old (thing, place)	ya'shan
obscene	m'gu'ne		
observant (religious, Jewish)	sho'mer mits'vot	oldtimer	va'teek
		oleander	har'duf
		olive	za'yeet
observant (perceptive)	p'ku'ach eye'in	omelette	cha'veeta
		omission	hash'ma'ta
obstinate	ak'shan	on	al
obtain (v.)	l'ha'seeg	once	pa'am
occasion	hiz'dam'nut	one	e'chad; a'chat
occupy (v.)	lit'fos	onion	ba'tsal
odd	mu'zar	only	rak
odor	rai'ach	onward	ka'deema
of	shel	opal	le'shem
offend (v.)	l'ha'a'leev	open	pa'tu'ach
offense	el'bon	operation (surgery)	ni'tu'ach
offer	ha'tsa'a		
office	mis'rad	opinion	de'a
officer (military)	ka'tseen	opponent	ya'reev
		opportunity	hiz'dam'nut

oppose (v.)   **oxygen**

oppose (v.)	l'hit'na'gued	ostrich	ya'en
opposite	mul	other	a'cher
option	brai'ra	out (doors)	ha'chuts'a
orange	ta'puz	outbreak	hit'par'tsut
orange grove	par'des	outcome	to'tsa'a
orange juice	mits ta'puzeem	outdated	m'yu'shan
orchard	bu'stan	outgoing	chav'ru'tee
orchestra	tiz'mo'ret	outing	ti'yul
orchid	sach'lav	outlook	hash'ka'fa
order	se'der	outside of...	chuts mi...
order (v.)	l'haz'meen	outstanding	bo'let
ordinance	p'ku'da	oven	ta'nur
ordinary	ra'gueel	overcast	m'u'nan
organ (pipe)	u'gav	overcoat	m'eel el'yon
organ (physio-logical)	e'ver	overnight	bin-leye'la
		overseas	me'ever la'yam
organization	ir'gun	overt	ga'lu'ee
orient	miz'rach	owl	yan'shuf
origin	ma'kor	ownership	ba'alut
oriole	za'havan	ox	shor
orphan	ya'tom	oxygen	cham'tsan

P

pacify (v.)	l'har'guee'a	paradise	gan e'den
pack	cha'vee'la	parallel	mak'beel
pack (v.)	le'eroz, lits'ror	paralysis	shi'tuk
page	a'mud	parasol	shim'shee'ya
pail	d'lee	parchment	k'laf
pain	k'ev	pardon	m'chee'la
paint	tse'va	parents	ho'reem
paint (v.)	li'tsa'yer	park	gan tsi'bu'ree
painting (artistic)	tsi'yur	park (v.)	la'cha'not
		parking lot	mig'rash cha'nee'ya
pair	zug		
pale	chi'ver	parliament (in Israel)	k'ne'set
palm (tree)	de'kel, ta'mar		
palm (of hand)	kaf yad	parlor	trak'leen
pamper (v.)	l'fa'nek	parrot	tu'kee
pamphlet	a'lon	parsley	kar'pas n'ha'rot
pan	ma'cha'vat	parsnip	gue'zer la'van
pancreas	lavlav	part	che'lek
panic	be'hala	particular	m'yu'chad
panorama	nof	partner	shu'taf
paper	n'yar	party (political)	mif'la'ga
paper clip	m'ha'dek		
paprika	pil'pelet	party (celebra-tion)	m'see'ba
parable	ma'shal		
parachute	mats'nai'ach		
parade	mits'ad, ta'ha'lucha	pass (v.)	la'a'vor
		passage	ma'a'var

48

passenger   **persimmon**

passenger	no'sai'a	peel	k'leepa
Passover	pe'sach	pen (for	et
passport	dar'kon	writing)	
past	a'var	fountain	
paste	de'vek	pen	et no'vai'a
pastry	u'guee'ya	penalty	o'nesh
pastry shop	mig'da'nee'ya	pencil	i'pa'ron
patch	t'leye	pendant	tach'sheet
path	mas'lul, de'rech		ta'lu'ee
patience	sav'la'nut	penknife	o'lar
patient	cho'le	pension	kits'ba,
(medical)			pen'see'ya
patron	to'mech	penthouse	deer'at gag
pauper	kab'tsan	people	am; a'na'sheem
pause	haf'sa'ka	pep	me'rets
pay (v.)	l'sha'lem	pepper	pil'pel
payment	tash'lum	peppermint	na'a'na
pea	a'fu'na	percent	a'chuz
peace	sha'lom	perfect	sha'lem,
hello or			mu'shlam
goodbye	sha'lom	perfidy	b'guee'da
peaceful	sha'ket, sha'lev	perfume	bo'sem
peach	a'far'sek	perhaps	u'leye
peacock	ta'vas	peril	sa'ka'na
peak	see, pis'ga	period (time)	t'ku'fa
peanut	bo'ten	period (punc-	n'kuda
pear	a'gas	tuation)	
pearl	mar'ga'leet,	permanent	ka'vu'a
	p'neena	permission	r'shut
pedagogue	m'cha'nech	permit	rish'yon
peddler	ro'chel	persecution	r'dee'fa
pedestrian	ho'lech re'guel	persimmon	a'far'simon

person	ben-adam, e'nosh	pilot	ta'yas
personal	p'ra'tee	pimple	cha'tat
personality	eeshi'yut	pin	see'ka
perspire (v.)	l'ha'zee'a	pinch	ts'veeta
persuade (v.)	l'shach'nai'a	pine (tree)	o'ren
pharmacist	ro'kai'ach	pineapple	a'nanas
pharmacy	bait mirka'chat	pink	va'rod
phase	sha'lav	pioneer	cha'luts
philanthropist	nad'van	pious	a'duk
phone (v.)	l'tal'fen, l'tsaltsel	pipe (plumbing)	tsi'nor
photo	tats'lum	pipe (smoking)	mik'te'ret
photographer	tsa'lam	pistol	ek'dach
physical (adj.)	gash'mee	pit	bor
physician	ro'fe	pitcher	kad
piano	p'san'ter	pity	rach'ma'nut
piccolo	chaleelon	place	ma'kom
pick (v.)	liv'chor	place (v.)	la'seem, l'ha'nee'ach
pickle	m'lafi'fon cha'muts	plague	ma'gai'fa
picture	t'mu'na	plain	pa'shut
piece	cha'tee'cha	plaintiff	to'vai'a
piece (of bread)	p'rusa	plan	toch'neet
		plane (tree)	do'lev
piece (of paper)	cha'teecha	plant (flora)	tse'mach
		plant (v.)	lin'to'a
pig	cha'zeer	plaster	tee'ach
pigeon	yo'na	plate (on table)	tsa'la'chat
pilgrim	o'le re'guel	platform	ba'ma
pill	ka'dur, g'lula	play (v.)	l'sa'chek
pillow	kar	play (on stage)	ma'cha'ze
		play (game)	mis'chak

playpen   **premier (head of government)**

playpen	lul	portion	che'lek, ma'na
please (v.)	l'ha'not	position	ma'a'mad, ma'tsav
please (also means: you're welcome)	b'va'ka'sha	positive	chee'yu'vee
		positive (certain)	much'lat
pleasure	ha'na'a	postage stamp	bul
plenty	she'fa	postcard	g'lu'ya
pliers	melka'cha'yeem	post office	bait do'ar
plow (v.)	la'cha'rosh	pot	seer
plum	sha'zeef	potato	ta'pud
prune	sha'zeef sha'chor	pour (v.)	lish'poch
		powder (cosmetic)	pud'ra
plumber	insta'la'tor		
pocket	kees	power	ko'ach
poem	sheer	practical	ma'asee
poison	ra'al	praise (v.)	l'ha'lel
police	mish'ta'ra	pray (v.)	l'hit'pa'lel
policeman	sho'ter	prayer	t'fila
polish (v.)	lil'tosh, l'tsach'-tsai'ach	prayerbook (Jewish)	si'dur
		precise	m'du'yak
polite	m'nu'mas	prediction	ni'bu'ee
pomegranate	ri'mon	predominant	sho'let
pond	b'rai'cha	preeminent	da'gul
pool	a'gama, brai'cha	prefer (v.)	l'ha'deef
poor	dal, a'nee	preferable	a'deef
poplar	tsaf'tsafa	pregnant	ha'ra, b'he'ra'yon
popular	a'ma'mee, a'hud		
porch	mir'pe'set	premier (head of government)	rosh-mem'-sha'la
port	na'mal		
porter	sa'bal		

51

prescription (doctor's) **proselyte (to Judaism)**

prescription (doctor's)	mir'sham	privilege	z'chut
present (tense)	ho've	prize	p'ras
present (gift)	ma'ta'na	problem	b'a'ya
present (introduce) (v.)	l'hatseeg	process	ta'ha'leech
		prodigy	ee'lu'ee
preserves (fruit)	ree'ba	produce (v.) (theatrical)	l'ha'feek
president	na'see	produce (edibles)	y'vul
press (v.) (iron)	l'ga'hets	product	totsar, mu'tsar
press (v.)	lil'chots	profession (vocation)	mik'tso'a
press (media)	ito'nut	profit	re'vach
presume (v.)	l'ha'nee'ach	profit (v.) (to earn)	l'har'vee'ach
pretty	nech'ma'da, ya'fa (f.)	profound	a'mok
prevent (v.)	lim'no'a	program	toch'neet
previous	ko'dem	progress	hit'kad'mut
price	m'cheer	prolific	sho'fai'a
pride	ga'ava	promenade	ta'ye'let
prime minister	rosh memsha'la	prominent	ya'du'a
primrose	ra'ke'fet	promise	hav'ta'cha
prince (ss)	na'seech, n'see'cha	pronunciation	miv'ta
		proof	ho'cha'cha
principle	i'ka'ron	proofreader	ma'guee'ha
printer	mad'pees	propaganda	ta'a'mula
prison	bait so'har	proper	ha'gun
private	ee'shee, p'ratee	property	r'chush
private (in army)	tu'ra'ee	prophet	na'vee
		proselyte (to Judaism)	guer (m.), g'yoret (f.)

proselyte (from Judaism)   **python**

proselyte (from Judaism)	m'shu'mad	public	pum'bee, tsi'bu'ree
		publicity	pir'so'met
prospect	si'ku'ee	publisher	mo'tsee l'or
prosperity	sig'sug, she'fa		(*acronym*: mol)
prostitute	zo'na		
protection	sh'mee'ra	pudding	cha'vee'tsa
protest	m'cha'a	pull (v.)	lim'shoch
proverb	ma'shal, pit'gam	pullet	par'gueet
		pulse	do'fek
provide (v.)	l'sa'pek	pump	mash'ai'va
proxy	ba ko'ach	pumpkin	d'la'at
prudent	za'heer	punctual	dak'di'kan
prune	sha'zeef sha'chor	purse	ar'nak
		push (v.)	lid'chof
Psalms	t'hi'leem	puzzle	chee'da
pub (bar)	mees'ba	python	pe'ten

Q

quality	ai'chut	question	sh'aila
quantity	ka'mut	queue	tor
quarrel	reev	quick	ma'heer
quarter	re'va	quiet	she'ket
(one-fourth)		quilt	ke'set
quarter	ro'va	quit (v.)	lin'tosh, la'a'zov
(section)		quiz	miv'chan
queen	mal'ka	quorum	min'yan
quest	chee'pus	quote (v.)	l'tsa'tet

R

rabbi	rav, ra'bee	ray	ke'ren
rabbit	ar'nav	razor	ta'ar
rabble	a'saf'suf	razor blade	sa'keen gui'lu'ach
race (running)	mai'rots		
race (identity)	gue'za	reach (v.)	l'ha'guee'a
racket	ra'ash	reaction	t'gu'va
radiant	zo'her	read (v.)	lik'ro
radical	kee'tso'nee	reader	ko're
radish	ts'non, ts'no'neet	ready	mu'chan
		real	ma'mashee
raffle	hag'ra'la	reality	m'tsee'ut
rag	s'mar'tut	reap (v.)	lik'tsor
rage	za'am	rear (v.)	l'ga'del
railway	m'silat-bar'zel	rear	a'chor
rain	gue'shem	reason (cause)	see'ba
rainbow	ke'shet	reason (rationality)	higa'yon, se'chel
raincoat	m'eel gue'shem		
raise (v.)	l'ha'reem	rebel	mo'red
raisin	tsee'muk	rebuke	to'cha'cha
rally	ki'nus	receipt	ka'ba'la
ranch	cha'va	receive (v.)	l'ka'bel
rape	o'nes	recipe	mat'kon
rapid	ma'heer	recognize	l'ha'keer
rare	na'deer	recommenda- tion	ham'la'tsa
rash (skin)	tif'ra'chat		
rat	ach'brosh	record (musical)	tak'leet
raw	gol'mee		

record   **resign (v.)**

record	r'shee'ma	relaxing (adj.)	mar'pe
record holder	ba'al see	release (v.)	l'shach'rer
recreation	bi'dur	religion	dat
recuperation	ha'cha'la'ma	religious	da'tee
red	a'dom	rely (v.)	lis'moch
redemption	g'ula	remark	he'ara
redhead	ad'mo'nee;	remember (v.)	liz'kor
	"gin'gee"	memory	zi'karon
reduce (v.)	l'tsamtsem,	remind (v.)	l'haz'keer
	l'hak'teen	renew (v.)	l'cha'desh
reduce (v.)	la're'det	rent	d'mai
(dieting)	b'mish'kal		s'chee'rut
reference book	se'fer ya'ats	repair	ti'kun
referendum	mish'al am	reparations	pee'tsu'yeem
reflect (v.)	l'har'her	replica	he'taik
(think)		reply	t'shuva
reflection	ha'cha'zara	report	duch, di'vuch
(light)		represent (v.)	l'ya'tseg
refrigerator	m'ka'rer	representative	na'tseeg
refuge	mik'lat	reptile	zo'chail
refugee	pa'leet	repulsive	mag'eel
refund	ha'cha'za'rat	request	ba'ka'sha
	tash'lum	requirement	d'reesha
refusal	sai'ruv	rescind (v.)	l'va'tel
refuse (trash)	p'so'let	rescue (v.)	l'ha'tseel
regime	mish'tar	research	mech'kar
regiment	g'dud	resemblance	deem'yon
region	ai'zor	reservation	ma'kom
registration	ri'shum		sha'mur
regret	cha'ra'ta	reside (v.)	la'gur
regular	sa'deer	resident	to'shav
relative(s)	ka'rov,	resign (v.)	l'hit'pa'ter
	k'ro'veem		

resort   **robe**

resort	m'kom mar'go'a	ride (v.)	lir'kov, lin'so'a
respect (v.)	l'ka'bed	ride	ti'yul
respect	ka'vod	ridicule	la'ag
respectable	nich'bad	rifle	ro've
responsible	ach'ra'ee	right (adj.) (correct)	na'chon
rest	m'nu'cha		
restaurant	mis'a'da	right (direction)	ya'meen
restroom	cha'dar no'chee'yut		
		righteous	tsa'deek
result	to'tsa'a	rightist (political)	y'ma'nee
retail	keem'o'nee		
retain (v.)	l'ha'cha'zeek	rind	k'rum
retire (to sleep) (v.)	lish'kav li'shon	ring (circle)	i'gul
		ring (for finger)	ta'ba'at
return (v.)	la'cha'zor		
return ticket	kar'tees ha'loch v'cha'zor	ring (phone call)	tsil'tsul
		rinse	sh'tee'fa
reveal (v.)	l'ga'lot	riots	p'ra'ot
revenge	n'ka'ma	rip	ke'ra
revenue	hach'na'sa	ripe	ba'shail
reverse (v.)	la'ha'foch	rise (v.)	la'kum
revival	t'chee'ya	risky	m'su'kan
revolution	ma'pai'cha	rite	te'kes
revolve (v.)	l'his'to'vev	rival	mit'cha're
reward	g'mul	river	na'har
rheumatism	shee'ga'ron	road	k'veesh
rhythm	ke'tsev	roam (v.)	lin'dod
rib	tse'la	roast (v.)	lits'lot
ribbon	se'ret	roasted	tsa'lu'ee
rice	o'rez	robbery	shod, g'nai'va
rich	a'sheer	robe	cha'luk
riddle	chee'da		

rock	se'la, e'ven	rubber band	gu'mee'ya
rocket	teel	rubbish	ash'pa
role	taf'keed	ruby	o'dem
roll (v.)	l'hit'gal'guel	rude	gas
roll (edible)	lach'ma'nee'ya	rug	sha'tee'ach
roof	gag	ruin	chur'ban
room	che'der	rule	k'lal; ta'kana
root	sho'resh	rule (v.)	lish'lot
rope	che'vel	ruler (on a	sar'gail
rose	ve'red; sho'shana	desk)	
rouge	o'dem	rumor	sh'mu'a
round (adj.)	a'gol	run (v.)	la'ruts
rouse (v.)	l'ha'eer	run	ree'tsa
route	na'teev	run (in	ke'ra
routine	shig'ra	stocking)	
row (of seats)	shu'ra	runway	mas'lul ham'ra'a
row	m'ree'va	rupture	she'ver
row (v.)	la'cha'tor	rust	cha'lu'da
(a boat)		rustic	kaf'ree
rowdy	pe're a'dam	ruthless	ach'za'ree
rub (v.)	l'shaf'shef	rye	shee'fon
rubber	gu'mee	rye whiskey	vis'kee shee'fon

S

Sabbath	sha'bat	sand	chol
Good		sandwich	ka'reech
Sabbath	sha'bat sha'lom	sanitary	b'ree'u'tee
sable	tso'vel	sanity	sh'fee'ut
sabotage	cha'ba'la	sapling	sha'teel
sacred	ka'dosh	sardine	ta'reet
sacrifice	kor'ban	satiate (v.)	l'has'bee'a
sad	a'tsuv	satisfy (v.)	l'sa'pek
safe (adj.)	ba'tu'ach	Saturday	sha'bat
safe	ka'se'fet	sauce	ro'tev
safety	bi'ta'chon	sauerkraut	k'ruv ka'vush
safety belt	cha'go'rat	sausage	nak'neek
	b'tee'chut	save (v.)	
sail	mif'ras	(rescue)	l'hatseel
sailing	sha'yeet,	save (v.)	la'chasoch
	haf'la'ga	(money)	
sailor	ma'lach,	savor	ta'am
	ya'meye	saw (in car-	ma'sor
salary	mas'ko'ret	pentry)	
sale	m'chee'ra	saying	mim'ra
salmon	il'teet	scale	moz'na'yeem
salt	me'lach	scalp	kar'ke'fet
salt shaker	mim'la'cha	scar	tsa'le'ket
salutation	b'racha	scarce	lo mas'peek
salve	mish'cha	scare (v.)	l'haf'cheed
same	do'me	scarf	su'dar, tsa'eef
sample	dug'ma	scent	rai'ach

schedule   **separate (adj.)**

schedule	lu'ach z'maneem	secondary	bait se'fer
scholar	m'lu'mad	school	tee'chon
school	bait se'fer	secondhand	m'shu'mash
science	ma'da	secret	sod
scissors	mis'pa'ra'yeem	secretary	maz'keer (m.),
scorpion	a'krav		maz'keera (f.)
Scotch	vis'kee skotch	sect	kat
(whiskey)		secular	chee'lo'nee
scratch	gue'rud	sedative	sam mar'guee'a
scream	ts'vacha	see (v.)	lir'ot
screw	bo'reg	seed	ze'ra
screwdriver	mav'reg	seize	lit'fos
scribe	so'fer	seldom	l'eeteem
scripture	kit'vai		r'cho'kot
	ha'ko'desh	select (v.)	liv'chor
scroll	m'gueela	self-employed	ats'ma'ee
sculpture	pe'sel	selfish	a'nochee'yee
sea	yam	self-service	mis'edet she'rut
seagull	sha'chaf	restaurant	ats'mee
seal	cho'temet	sell (v.)	lim'kor
seal (animal)	ke'lev yam	seltzer	so'da
seamstress	to'fe'ret	send (v.)	lish'lo'ach
search (v.)	l'cha'pes	seniors	z'ke'neem
searchlight	zar'kor	(elderly)	
sea shell	kon'cheet	sensation	t'chu'sha
sea shore	chof yam	sense	chush, re'guesh;
season	o'na		se'chel
seasoning	tav'leen	sensible	na'von
seat	mo'shav	sensitive	ra'gueesh
second	she'nee	sentence	mish'pat
second (in	shnee'ya	sentry	za'keef
time)		separate (adj.)	nif'rad

serene	sha'lev	shed	ts'reef
sergeant	sa'mal	sheep	tson
series	sid'ra	sheet (bedding)	sa'deen
serious	r'tsee'nee	sheet (paper)	guila'yon
sermon	d'rasha	shelf	ma'daf
serpent	na'chash	shelter	mik'lat
servant	m'sha'ret	shepherd	ro'e
serve (v.)	l'sha'ret	shield	ma'guen
service	she'rut	shin	shok
session	ye'shiva	shine (v.)	liz'ro'ach
settle (an argument) (v.)	l'ya'shev	shiny	mav'reek
		ship	o'nee'ya
settle (in a place) (v.)	l'hit'ya'shev	shirt	ku'to'net
		shiver (v.)	lir'od
settlement (community)	yi'shuv	shock	he'lem
		shoe (s)	na'al (a'yeem)
seven	she'va	shoelace	s'roch na'al
seventeen	sh'va esrai	shoemaker	sandlar
seventy	shiv'eem	shoot (v.)	li'rot b...
severe	cha'mur	shop (store)	cha'nut
sew (v.)	lit'for	shopkeeper	chen'va'nee
sex	meen	short	ka'tsar
sexton	sha'mash	shortage	mach'sar
shade	tsel	short change	na'tan o'def
shame	bu'sha, cher'pa		pa'chot
shape	tsu'ra	short circuit	ke'tser
share	che'lek	shortcoming	chee'sa'ron
sharp	chad; cha'reef	shortly	b'ka'rov
shave (v.) (oneself)	l'hit'ga'lai'ach	shorts	mich'ni'sa'- yeem k'tsa'reem
shave	gui'lu'ach		
she	hee	shot (from gun)	yi'ree'ya

shot (injection)   **sky**

shot (injection)	z'ree'ka	silver	ke'sef
shoulder	ka'tef	similar	do'me
shout (v.)	lits'ok	simple	pa'shut
shove (v.)	lid'chof	sin	chet
shovel	ya'e, et	sincere	a'mee'tee
show (v.)	l'har'ot	sing (v.)	la'sheer
show (theatrical)	ha'tsa'ga	singer	za'mar
		single	ya'cheed, bo'ded
shower	mik'la'chat	single (unmarried)	lo na'su'ee
shower (v.)	l'hit'ka'lai'ach		
shower (light rain)	mim'tar	sink	kee'yor
		sip	l'guee'ma
shrewd	pi'ke'ach	sir	a'don
shrub	see'ach	siren (alarm)	tso'far az'a'ka
shut (v.) (eyes)	la'atsom	sirloin	b'sar mo'ten
shut (v.)	lis'gor	sister	a'chot
shutters	t'ree'seem	sister-in-law	guee'sa
shy	beye'shan	sit (v.)	la'she'vet
sick	cho'le	situation	ma'tsav
sickness	ma'cha'la	six	shesh
side	tsad	sixteen	shesh esrai
sidewalk	mid'racha	sixty	shisheem
sideways	ha'tsee'da	size	mee'da
sigh	a'na'cha	skate (v.)	l'ha'cha'leek
sightseer	ta'yar	skillful	much'shar
sign (v.)	la'cha'tom	skim milk	cha'lav ra'ze
sign (hint)	see'man	skin	or
sign (placard)	she'let	skinny	ka'chush, ra'ze
silence	sh'tee'ka	skip (v.)	l'da'leg
silent	sho'tek	skirt	cha'tsa'eet
silk	me'shee	skullcap	ki'pa
silly	tip'shee	sky	sha'ma'yeem

62

slave   **sound**

slave	e'ved	social	chev'ra'tee
sleep	she'na	society	chevra
sleep (v.)	li'shon	sock(s)	gue'rev,
sleeve	shar'vul		gar'ba'yeem
slice	p'rusa	soda	ga'zoz
slice of		sofa	sa'pa
bread	pat le'chem	soft	rach, a'deen
slight (adj.)	dak, kal	soft-boiled egg	baitsa ra'ka
slime	teet	soil	kar'ka, a'dama
slipper	na'al ba'yeet	soil (v.)	l'lachlech
slow	ee'tee	solace	ne'chama
slowly	l'at, l'at	solar	shimshee
small	ka'tan, pa'ut	soldier	cha'yal
small change	ke'sef ka'tan	sole (of foot)	kaf re'guel
smart (shrewd)	pik'chee	sole (v.)	l'hatkeen
smell	rai'ach		su'lee'ya
smelling salts	milchai	solution	pit'ron
	ha'ra'cha	some	ma'she'hu;
smile	chi'yuch		ai'ze; ka'ma
smoke	a'shan	sometimes	lif'a'meem
smoke (v.)	l'a'shen	son	ben
smooth	cha'lak	song	sheer
snack	a'ru'cha ka'la	son-in-law	cha'tan
snake	na'chash	sophisticated	m'tuch'kam
snapdragon	lo'a ha'aree	sore (adj.)	ko'ev
sneaker	na'al hit'amlut	sore	pe'tsa
sneeze	ee'tush	sorrow	tsa'ar
sniffle	na'ze'let	sorry	mits'ta'er
snow	she'leg	sort	sug
soap	sa'bon	so-so	kacha'kacha
soccer	ka'dur re'guel	soul	n'sha'ma
sociable	chav'ru'tee	sound	kol, ts'leel

sound (adj.) | spunk

sound (adj.)	ba'ree	speed	m'hee'rut
soup	ma'rak	spend (v.) (money)	l'ho'tsee ke'sef
sour	cha'muts		
source	ma'kor	spend (v.) (time)	l'va'lot
south	da'rom		
souvenir	maz'ke'ret	spicy	m'tu'bal
space (room)	merchav, ma'kom	spider	a'ka'veesh
		spigot	be'rez
space (extraterrestrial)	cha'lal	spill (v.)	lish'poch
		spinach	te'red
		spine	shid'ra
space ship	cha'la'leet	spirit	ru'ach
spacious	m'ru'vach	spiritual	ru'cha'nee
Spain	s'farad	spit (v.)	li'rok
spare (part)	cha'laf	splendor	hod, ha'dar
spark	nee'tsots	splinter	sh'vav, r'sees
sparrow	d'ror	split (v.)	l'hit'pa'tsel
spasm	a'veet	split	pee'tsul
spatula	ma'reet	spoil (v.)	l'kal'kel
speak (v.)	l'da'ber	sponge	s'fog
speaker	no'em	spoon (table)	kaf
spearmint	na'a'na	spoon (tea)	ka'peet
special	m'yu'chad	spouse	ben'zug; ba'al (m.); ee'sha (f.)
specialist	mum'che		
specific	m'su'yam		
specimen	dug'ma	sprain	m'tee'chat-e'ver
speck	ke'tem	spring (season)	a'veev
spectacle	macha'ze	spring (jump) (v.)	lik'fots
spectator	tso'fe		
speech	di'bur	spring (water source)	ma'ayan
speech (an address)	n'um		
		spunk	o'mets

spy	m'ra'guel	state	ma'tsav
squander (v.)	l'vazbez	(condition)	
square	ro'va	state of mind	ma'tsav ru'ach
(location)		station (depot)	ta'cha'na
square (adj.)	ra'vu'a	stationery	mach'shee'rai
squeeze (v.)	lil'chots		k'tee'va
squirrel	s'na'ee	station house	ta'cha'nat
stable (adj.)	ya'tseev	(police)	mish'ta'ra
stable	ur'va	statue	an'dar'ta; pe'sel
stack	a'rai'ma	status	ma'a'mad
stage	ba'ma, bee'ma	statute	chok
stairs	mad're'got	stay (v.)	l'hi'sha'er
stale	lo ta'ree,	steady	sa'deer, ka'vu'a
	m'yushan	steak	um'tsa
stammer (v.)	l'gamguem	steal (v.)	lig'nov
stamp	bul	steam	kee'tor
(postage)		steel	p'la'da
stand (v.)	la'a'mod	stenography	kats'ra'nut
standard of	ra'mat	step	tsa'ad
living	ha'cha'yeem	stepbrother	ach cho'reg
standing room	m'komot	stepdaughter	bat cho're'guet
	a'meeda	stepfather	av cho'reg
star	ko'chav	stepmother	em cho're'guet
starch	a'mee'lan	stepsister	a'chot
star of David	ma'guen		cho're'guet
	da'veed	stepson	ben cho'reg
start (v.)	l'hat'cheel	stern (adj.)	cha'mur
start	hat'cha'la	stew	tav'sheel
starving (adj.)	ra'ev	steward(ess)	da'yal,
state (country)	m'dee'na	(on plane)	da'ye'let
state (v.)	l'hats'heer	stewed fruit	liv'tan pai'rot
(declare)		stick	ma'kel

stick (v.)   **stupid**

stick (v.)	l'had'beek	strawberry	tut'sa'de
stiff	nuk'she	stream	na'chal
still (adj.)	do'mem	street	r'chov
still (adv.)	a'da'yeen, od	strength	ko'ach
stimulant	mam'reets	stress (pressure)	la'chats
sting	o'kets		
stingy	kam'tsan	stress (v.) (emphasize)	l'had'gueesh
stink (v.)	l'has'ree'ach		
stir (v.)	l'o'rer	stretch (v.)	lim'to'ach
stock (supply)	m'leye	stretcher	a'lunka
stock broker	sar'sur bur'sa	stricken	mu'ke
stock exchange	bur'sa	strict	m'du'yak
stomach	kai'va, be'ten	strife	sich'such, mach'lo'ket
stone	e'ven, se'la		
stoop (v.)	l'hit'ko'fef	strike (v.) (labor)	sh'vee'ta
stop (v.)	la'atsor		
storage	ach'sa'na	strike (v.) (to hit)	l'ha'kot, l'hat'keef
store (shop)	cha'nut		
stork	cha'see'da	string	chut
storm	s'a'ra	string bean	she'u'eet y'ru'ka
stormy	so'er	string instruments	k'lai mai'tar
story	si'pur		
stove	ta'nur	stripe	pas
straight	ya'shar	strong	cha'zak
strain (tension)	me'tach	struggle	ma'avak
strainer	mis'ne'net	stubborn	ak'shan
strange	mu'zar	stuck-up	m'nu'pach
stranger	zar	studio	ul'pan
strangle (v.)	l'cha'nek	study	li'mud
strap (belt)	r'tsu'a	study (v.)	lil'mod
straw (for drinking)	kash	stupendous	ka'beer
		stupid	m'tum'tam

style   **swamp**

style	sig'non	sundown	sh'kee'at ha'cha'ma
style (fashion)	of'na	sundries	sho'not
subject	no'sai	sunflower	cha'ma'neet
submarine	tso'lelet	sunglasses	mish'ki'fai she'mesh
submit (v.)	l'ha'gueesh		
subscribe (v.)	la'cha'tom, li'trom	sunrise	z'reechat ha'she'mesh
substitute	m'ma'lai ma'kom	superficial	shit'chee
		superfluous	m'yu'tar
subtract (v.)	l'cha'ser	supervise (v.)	l'hash'guee'ach
suburb	par'bar	supper	a'ruchat e'rev
succeed (v.)	l'hats'lee'ach	support	t'mee'cha
success	hats'la'cha	supposition	hash'ra'a
successive	ra'tsuf	sure	ba'tu'ach
suck (v.)	lim'tsots	surgeon	m'na'tai'ach
suddenly (adv.)	pit'om	surplus	o'def
suffer (v.)	lis'bol	surprise	haf'ta'a
suffering	se'vel	surrender	k'nee'a
sufficient	deye, mas'peek	survey	se'ker
sugar	su'kar	survivor	sa'reed
suggestion	ha'tsa'a	suspect (v.)	la'cha'shod
suit (apparel)	cha'lee'fa	suspect (adj.)	cha'shud
suit (judicial)	t'vee'a	suspend (v.)	lid'chot
sum	s'chum, sach ha'kol	suspenders (for trousers)	k'tai'fot
summary	si'kum	swaddling clothes (diapers)	chi'tu'leem
summer	ka'yeets		
summit	pis'ga		
sun	she'mesh		
sunburn	shee'zuf	swallow	s'nu'neet
sundae	g'lid'at pe'rot	swallow (v.)	liv'lo'a
Sunday	yom ri'shon	swamp	bee'tsa

swan   **system**

swan	bar'bur	sweet potato	ba'ta'ta
swap (v.)	l'ha'cha'leef	sweets	su'ka'ree'yot
swear(v.)	l'hash'bee'a	swim (v.)	lis'chot
sweat	ze'a	swimming	s'chee'ya
sweat (v.)	l'ha'zee'a	swimming pool	braichat
sweater	a'fu'da		s'chee'ya
sweep (v.)	l'ta'te	swimsuit	be'gued yam
sweeper	m'ta'te	swindle	hona'a, ra'ma'ut
(broom)		sword	che'rev
sweepstakes	hag'ra'la	symbol	se'mel
sweet (adj.)	ma'tok	sympathetic	o'hed
sweeten (v.)	l'ham'teek	(adj.)	
sweetheart	a'huv (m.),	(supportive)	
	a'huva (f.)	synagogue	bait k'ne'set
sweet pea	a'funa	syringe	maz'rek
	rai'cha'neet	system	shee'ta

T

table	shulchan	taxi	mo'neet
tablecloth	mapat shul'chan	tea	tai
tack	na'ats	teach (v.)	l'la'med
tail	za'nav	teacher (m.) (f.)	mo're, mo'ra
tailor	cha'yat		
take (v.)	la'ka'chat	tea kettle	kumkum tai
takeoff (from runway)	ham'ra'a	team (in sports)	k'vutsa
		team (of horses)	tse'med
tale	ma'asee'ya		
talent	kish'ron	team (crew)	tse'vet
talk	see'cha	tear (from eye)	dim'a
tall	ga'vo'ha	tear (v.)	lik'ro'a
tame (adj.)	m'ulaf, m'vu'yat	teen years	sh'not ha'esrai
tangerine	man'direena	teeny	ka'ton
tangible	mu'cha'shee	telegram	miv'rak
tape (recording)	se'ret (l'hak'la'ta)	telephone (v.)	l'tal'fen
		tell (v.)	l'sa'per
tardy	m'a'cher	teller (in bank)	ku'pa'ee
target	ma'ta'ra	temper	mats'av ru'ach
tart (adj.)	cha'muts, cha'reef	temperature	mee'dat ha'chom
task	taf'keed, m'see'ma	temple (Holy Temple)	bait hamikdash
taste	ta'am	temple (synagogue)	bait k'ne'set
tasty	ta'eem		
tasteless	ta'fel	temple (part of head)	ra'ka
tax	mas		

tempo   **thumb**

tempo	ke'tsev	these	ai'le
temporary	z'manee	thick	a've
ten	e'ser	thief	ga'nav
tenant	so'cher	thigh	ya'rech
Ten Com-	a'seret	thimble	etsba'on
mandments	ha'dibrot	thin	dal
tendency	m'ga'ma,	thin (person)	ra'ze
	n'tee'ya	thing	da'var, che'fets
tender	rach, a'deen	think (v.)	la'cha'shov
tenet	i'karon	third	shleeshee
tense (adj.)	ma'tu'ach	thirsty	tsa'me
tent	o'hel	thirteen	shlosh esrai
termination	si'yum, g'mar	thirty	shlo'sheem
terrace	mir'pe'set	this	ze (m.), zot (f.)
terrible	a'yom	thorough	ma'keef
test	miv'chan,	though	lam'rot
	ni'sa'yon	thought	mach'sha'va
test (v.)	liv'dok	thousand	e'lef
testimony	e'dut	two thousand	al'pa'yeem
textbook	se'fer li'mud	thread	chut
thanks, thank	to'da, to'da	threaten (v.)	l'a'yem
you	ra'ba	three	sha'losh
thankful	a'seer to'da	thrifty	ches'cho'nee
Thanksgiving	yom ha'hoda'ya	thrilling	mar'teet
Day		thrive (v.)	l'sag'seg
theft	g'nai'va	throat	ga'ron
then	az, l'fee'chach	throng	ha'mon
therapy	reepoo'ee	throw (v.)	liz'rok
there	sham	throw out	l'hash'leech
therefore	la'chen	(v.)	
thermometer	mach'dom	thug	sa'keen'a'ee
thermos	sh'mar'chom	thumb	a'gu'dal;
			bo'hen

70

thunder   **total**

thunder	ra'am	toilet	bait ki'sai
thunderbolt	ba'rak	toilet articles	k'lai tam'ruk
Thursday	yom	toilet water	mai bo'sem
	cha'mee'shee	token	ot, see'man,
thus	kach, kacha		se'mel
ticket	kar'tees	tolerance	sav'la'nut
ticket window	esh'nav	tomato	ag'va'nee'ya
	kar'tee'seem	tomb	ke'ver
tickle (v.)	l'dag'deg	tomorrow	ma'char
tidy (adj.)	m'su'dar, na'kee	in two days	moch'ro'ta'-
tie (v.)	l'ka'sher,		yeem
	l'cha'bel	tone	ts'leel
tie (apparel)	a'neeva	tongue	la'shon
tiger	na'mer	tonight	ha'leyela
tight (adj.)	ha'duk	tonsil	sha'ked
tile	ra'af	too	gam
time	z'man	tool	k'lee,
time (period)	t'ku'fa		mach'sheer
timetable	lu'ach z'maneem	tooth	shen
timid	beye'sha'nee	teeth	shi'na'yeem
tin	pach	tooth paste	mish'chat
tint	ga'ven		shi'na'yeem
tiny	za'eer	tooth ache	k'ev shen
tire (v.)	l'hit'ya'ef	toothbrush	miv're'shet
tire (on	tsa'meeg		shi'na'yeem
vehicle)		torch	la'peed
tire pressure	la'chats	torch	pa'nas kees
	ts'mee'gueem	(flashlight)	
title	ko'te'ret, to'ar	tortoise	tsav
today	ha'yom	torture	eenu'ee
toe	ets'ba ha're'guel	tot	pa'ot
together	ya'chad	total	sach ha'kol

71

touch (v.)   **turkey**

touch (v.)	lin'go'a, l'ma'shesh	transit	ma'a'var
touch (one's heart)	no'gai'a la'lev	translate (v.)	l'tar'guem
		translation	tir'gum
tough	ka'she	transportation	ho'va'la
tour	tee'yul	trap	mal'ko'det
tourist	ta'yar	trash can	pach ash'pa
toward	k'la'pai, lik'rat	tremble (v.)	lir'od
towel	ma'gue'vet	trend	m'gama
tower	mig'dal	trial (in court)	mish'pat
towing service (for vehicle)	she'rut g'ree'ra	triangle	m'shu'lash
		tribe	she'vet
toxic	mar'eel	trip	n'see'a
toy	tsa'a'tsu'a	triumph	nits'a'chon
track (v.)	la'a'kov	trouble (v.)	l'hat'ree'ach
trade (vocation)	u'ma'nut, mik'tso'a	troubles	tsa'rot, d'a'got
		troupe (musical)	la'ha'ka
trade	mis'char		
trader	so'cher	trousers	michni'sa'yeem
tradition	ma'so'ret	truck	ma'sa'eet
traffic	t'nu'a (ba'derech)	true (adj.)	a'mee'tee; na'chon
traffic jam	p'kak t'nu'a	trumpet	cha'tso'tsra
traffic light	ram'zor	trust	ai'mun
traffic sign	tam'rur	truth	e'met
trail	sh'veel	try (v.)	l'na'sot, l'hish'ta'del
train (v.)	l'a'men		
train (railroad)	ra'ke'vet	Tuesday	yom shleeshee
trait	o'fee	tuition	s'char li'mud
traitor	bo'gued	tulip	tsi'vo'nee
transfer	ha'a'vara	tumor	guee'dul
transgression	a've'ra	tunnel	min'ha'ra
		turkey	tar'ni'gol ho'du

turn	si'buv	two	sh'tai;
turn (on line)	tor		sh'teye'eem
turnip	le'fet	twosome	zug
tweezer	mal'ket	type	ti'pus
twelve	sh'taim esrai	typical	ti'pu'see
twenty	es'reem	typewriter	m'cho'nat
twice	pa'a'meye'eem		k'teeva
twin(s)	te'om(eem)	tyrant	ro'dan, a'reets
twisted (adj.)	a'kum	tyro	tee'ron

U

ugly	m'cho'ar	undoubtedly	b'lee sa'fek
ulcer	ul'kus	undress (v.)	l'haf'sheet,
ultimate	so'fee		l'hit'pa'shet
umbrella	mit'ree'ya	unemployed	muv'tal
umpire	bo'rer, sho'fet	unemployment	av'ta'la
unanimous	pe e'chad	unequal	lo sha've
uncivilized	pe're	uneven	lo ya'shar
uncle	dod	unexpected	lo tsa'fu'ee
uncommon	bil'tee ra'gueel	unfair	lo ho'guen
unconditional	b'lee t'na'eem	unfaithful	lo ne'e'man
unconscious	cha'sar ha'ka'ra	unfamiliar	lo ya'du'a
under	ta'chat	unfasten (v.)	l'ha'teer
underbrush	see'cheem	unfinished	lo ga'mur
underclothes	l'va'neem,	unfit	lo ra'u'ee
	tach'to'neem	unfortunate	mis'ken, um'lal
undercover	so'dee	unfriendly	lo ye'dee'du'tee
underdone	lo m'vushal deye	unfurnished	lo m'ro'hat
undergraduate	stu'dent	ungentlemanly	lo m'nu'mas
underground	mach'te'ret,	unhappy	a'tsuv
	tat'kar'ka'ee	unharmed	lo nee'zok
undersea	tat'ya'mee	unhealthy	lo ba'ree
undershirt	gufee'ya	unholy	lo ka'dosh
understand (v.)	l'ha'veen	unification	ee'chud
understanding	bee'na, ha'va'na	uniform	ma'deem
undesirable	lo ra'tsu'ee	unify (v.)	l'a'ched
undo (v.)	l'ha'teer,	unimportant	lo cha'shuv
	l'ha'seer	unintelligible	lo mu'van

74

uninteresting

utterly

uninteresting	lo m'an'yen	update (v.)	l'ad'ken
unique	ya'cheed	upholsterer	ra'pad
	b'mee'no	upkeep	acha'za'ka
unit	y'chee'da	upright	y'shar de'rech;
United Nations	''um'' (acronym)		za'kuf
United States	artsot ha'breet	upset (adj.)	m'vul'bal,
unknown	lo no'da		nir'gaz
unleavened	ma'tsa	urban	ee'ro'nee
bread		urge (v.)	lid'chof
unload (v.)	lif'rok	urgent	da'chuf
unmarried	ra'vak (m.),	urinate (v.)	l'hash'teen
(person)	ra'va'ka (f.)	U.S.S.R.	b'reet
unnecessary	lo na'chuts		ha'mo'atsot
unoccupied	lo ta'fus	usage	no'hag,
unreal	lo ma'mashee		shi'mush
unripe	lo ba'shel	use (v.)	l'hish'ta'mesh
unsafe	lo ba'tu'ach,		b...; l'na'tsel
	m'su'kan	used	m'shu'mash
unsanitary	lo hig'yai'nee	useful	mo'eel
unsuccessful	lo muts'lach	usher	sad'ran
unsuitable	lo mat'eem	usually	b'de'rech k'lal
until	ad	utility (public)	she'rut
unusual	lo ra'gueel		tsee'bu'ree
up	al; l'ma'la	utterly	l'gam'rai
upbringing	chi'nuch,		
	guee'dul		

75

V

vacancy	ma'kom pa'nu'ee	venison	b'sar tsvee
vacant	raik, pa'nu'ee	venom	e'res, ra'al
vacation	cho'fesh, chuf'sha	ventilate (v.)	l'av'rer
		verdict	p'sak deen
vacuum (v.)	lish'ov a'vak	version	gueer'sa
vacuum	cha'lal raik	very	m'od
vagrant	na v'nad	vest	cha'zee'ya
vague	lo ba'rur	vestibule	mis'diron
vain	hav'lee, gav'ta'nee	veteran (adj.)	va'teek
		via	de'rech
validate (v.)	l'hash'reer	vial	tslo'cheet
valise	miz'va'da	vice versa	l'he'fech
valley	e'mek, bik'a	vicinity	s'vee'va
value	e'rech	vicious	m'ru'sha
vanilla	va'neel	victim	kor'ban
varied	sho'ne	victory	nitsa'chon
vase	a'gar'tel	view	hash'ka'fa
veal	b'sar e'guel	vigilant (adj.)	mash'guee'ach
veal chop	k'tee'tat e'guel	vigor	me'rets
vegetables	yira'kot	vile	sha'fal
vegetarian	tsim'cho'nee	vilify (v.)	l'hashmeets
vehicle	re'chev	village	k'far, mo'sha'va
veil	tsa'eef	villain	na'val
vein	va'reed, gueed	vindicate (v.)	l'hats'deek
velvet	k'tee'fa	vine	gue'fen
vengeance	nika'ma	vinegar	cho'mets

vineyard   **vulture**

vineyard	ke'rem	vocation	mik'tso'a
violence	a'lee'mut	voice	kol
violet	se'guel	voice (v.)	l'va'te,
violin	ki'nor		l'hash'mee'a
virgin	b'tu'la	void (adj.)	ba'tel
virtue	s'gu'la	volleyball	ka'dur af
virtuous	mu'sa'ree	volume (book)	ke'rech
visa	a'sha'ra	volunteer	mit'na'dev
vision	r'ee'ya	vomit (v.)	l'ha'kee
visit (v.)	l'va'ker	vote (v.)	liv'chor,
visit	bi'kur		l'hats'bee'a
visiting the ill	bi'kur cho'leem	vow	ne'der
visitor	o'rai'ach	voyage	n'see'a
vital	chee'yu'nee	vulgar	gas
vocabulary	ots'ar mi'leem	vulture	pe'res

77

W

wage	sa'char	washable	ka'vees
wager	hee'mur	washing	m'cho'nat
wagon	a'ga'la	machine	k'veesa
wail	kee'na	waste	bizbuz
waist	mo'ten	waste	sal p'so'let
wait (v.)	l'ham'teen	basket	
waiter,	mel'tsar,	watch (v.)	lish'mor
waitress	mel'tsa'reet	watch	sha'on
wake (v.)	l'ha'eer,	(timepiece)	
	l'hit'o'rer	watchmaker	sha'an
walk (v.)	la'le'chet	water	meye'yeem
walk	tee'yul b're'guel	waterfall	ma'pal
wall (interior)	keer		meye'yeem
wall (exterior)	cho'ma	watermelon	a'va'tee'ach
wallet	teek, ar'nak	wave (in	gal
walnut	e'go'za	ocean)	
walrus	sus-yam	microwave	mik'ro-gal
want (v.)	lir'tsot	oven	
war	mil'cha'ma	wax	sha'a'va, do'nag
wardrobe	a'ron b'ga'deem	we	a'nach'nu
warehouse	mach'san	weak	cha'lash
warm(th)	cham, chom	wealthy	a'sheer
warm (v.)	l'cha'mem	weapon	k'lee ne'shek
warning	az'ha'ra	wear (v.)	lil'bosh
wash (v.)	lir'chots,	wear a hat	la'cha'vosh
(people)	l'hit'ra'chets	(v.)	
wash (v.)	lich'bos	weasel	sa'mur
(laundry)			

78

weather	me'zeg a'veer
weaver	o'reg
web	re'shet
wedding	cha'tu'na
wedding ring	ta'ba'at n'su'een
Wednesday	yom r'vee'ee
week	sha'vu'a
two weeks	sh'vu'eye'eem
weekend	sof-sha'vu'a
weekly (publication)	sha'vu'on
weep (v.)	liv'kot
weigh (v.)	lish'kol
weight	mish'kal
welcome!	ba'ruch ha'ba!
well (for water)	b'er, ma'a'yan
well-off	a'meed
west	ma'arav
wet	lach, ra'tov
what	ma
wheat	chee'ta
wheel	galgal
steering wheel	he'gue
when	ka'asher, ma'teye
where	ai'fo
whisper (v.)	lil'chosh
whisper	la'chash

whistle	sh'ree'ka
white	la'van
white lie	she'ker la'van
who	mee
whole	sha'lem
wholesaler	see'to'na'ee
whore	zo'na
whose	shel mee
why	la'ma, ma'du'a
wicked	ra'sha
wide	ra'chav
widow(er)	al'mana, alman
wife	ee'sha
wig	pai'a noch'reet
wild (adj.)	pir'ee
will	ra'tson
willingly	b'ra'tson
wind	ru'ach
window	cha'lon
window shade	ma'sach cha'lon
window shutter	trees cha'lon
wine	ya'yeen
wing	ka'naf
wink	k'ree'tsa
winner	zo'che
winter	cho'ref
wipe (v.)	lin'gov
wire	ta'yeel
wisdom	choch'ma
wise	cha'cham, na'von

witch   **wrong**

witch	mach'she'fa	world	o'lam
with	im	worm	to'la
within	p'nee'ma	worry	d'a'ga
without (outside)	ba'chuts	worthwhile	k'deye
		wound	pe'tsa
without (missing)	b'lee	wrapper	a'tee'fa
		wreath	zer, a'tara
witness	ed	wreck	chur'ban
wolf	z'ev	wrestle (v.)	l'hit'a'bek
woman, women	ee'sha, na'sheem	wrinkle	ke'met
		wrist	pe'rek ha'yad
wonder (v.)	l'hit'pa'le	write (v.)	lich'tov
wonderful	nif'la	writer (author)	so'fer
wood	ets		
woodpecker	na'kar	writing	k'tee'va
wool	tse'mer	writing desk	mich'ta'va
word	mi'la	wrong (adj.)	lo na'chon, mut'e
work	a'vo'da		
worker	po'el, o'ved	wrong	a'vel, ee'tse'dek

X

xenophobia	sin'at za'-reem	X-ray	ke'ren rent'guen

Y

yam	ta'mus	yesterday	et'mol
yard	cha'tser	day before	
yarn	chut l'a'-ree'ga	yesterday	shil'shom
		yet	a'da'yeen, od
yawn	pi'hee'ka	you	a'ta (m.), at (f.)
year	sha'na	you (plural)	a'tem (m.), a'ten (f.)
yearly	sh'na'tee		
yell	tsa'a'ka	young	tsa'eer
yellow	tsa'hov	youngster	na'ar, ye'led
yes	ken	youth	n'u'reem

Z

zealot	ka'na'ee	Zion(ism)	tsee'yon(ut)
zenith	see	zipper	roch'san
zero	e'fes	zone	ai'zor
zinc	a'vats	zoo	gan cha'yot

A

a'bed (v.)	to process, adapt; cultivate	ad'eef	preferable, superior
ach(ot)	brother, sister	adeen	delicate, gentle, refined
achot	nurse	adeesh	apathetic
acharai	after	adlo'yada	Purim carnival
acharon	last	adom	red
achava	brotherhood	adon	Mr.; sir
achbar	mouse	ad'raba	on the contrary
ach'brosh	rat	adreechal	architect
achdut	unity	a'duk	religiously observant
ach'er	different, other		
achor	rear, in back	af	nose
achreye'ee	responsible	afar	dust
achshav	now	afarsek	peach
achuz	percentage	afars'mon	persimmon
achuza	estate	afeelu	although
achyan(eet)	nephew, niece	a'fel	dark, gloomy
achzaree	cruel	a'for	gray
achzava	disappointment	afuda	sweater
ad	until	afuna	pea
ad olam	forever	agada	legend, fable
adam	man; human being	agaf	wing, department
adama	soil; earth; land	agala	wagon, carriage
adasha	lentil; lens	agam	pond, lake
ada'yeen	still, yet	agas	pear

83

a'gueel	earring	almonee	anonymous
agudal	thumb	am	nation, people
agun(a)	deserted husband, wife	am ha'arets	ignoramus
		amal	hard labor
agvanee'ya	tomato	ama'mee	popular, folksy
ahada	sympathy, support	a'man	artist
		ambatya, ambat	bathtub, bath
ahava	love		
ahuv(a)	beloved (m.) (f.)	a'meet	colleague, associate
aich, aichut	how; quality		
ain davar!	never mind!	ameetee; emet	truthful; truth
aiz'e	which	a'na?	whereto?
akeret ba'yeet	housewife	ana (poetic)	if you please
a'kev	heel	anachnu	we
akleem	climate	a'naf	branch
akshan	stubborn	anak	giant; necklace
al	don't; on, above	anan	cloud
al kol paneem	at any rate	m'unan	cloudy
		anasheem	people
al lo davar!	don't mention it	anav	modest, humble
al n'kala	easily	anava	berry
al pe	by heart	andarta	statue; memorial sculpture
al shem	in name of; in memory of		
		a'nee	I
al yad	near	anee	poor
aleeya	ascent; immigration to Israel; honor at synagogue service	aneeva	necktie
		ara'ee	tentative
		arafel	fog
		arba	four
		arba-esrai	fourteen
		arba'eem	forty
alman(a)	widower, widow	a'ree	lion

a'reesa	cradle	atara	glory, crown, adornment
areets	tyrant		
argaman	purple	ateesha	sneeze
argaz	crate, box	a'teed	future
armon	palace	a'teek	ancient
arnak	purse, wallet	a'teekot	antiquities
arnav	rabbit	atsabeem	nerves
a'roch (adj.)	long	m'atsben (v.)	enervates
a'roch (v.)	to arrange, set up		
		a'tsel	lazy
a'rom	nude	atsma'ut	independence
aron	closet, cupboard	atsor (v.)	to stop
aruba	chimney	atsum	mighty, powerful
a'rum	sly		
a'rus(a)	betrothed (m.) (f.)	atsuv	sad
		av	father
a'seemon	token (for phone)	abba	dad
		avabu'a	blister
ash	moth	avak	dust; powder
a'sheer	wealthy	aval	but
a'shem	guilty	avar	past
a'shen (v.)	to smoke	avatee'ach	watermelon
ashan	smoke	avaz	goose
ashpa	rubbish	a've	coarse, thick
ashra'ee	credit	aveda	loss
a'son	disaster	avud	lost
asot (v.)	to make, to do; to perform	a'veer	air
		aveera	atmosphere
a'suk	busy, occupied	a'vel	evil
a'sur	forbidden	avnet	sash
at(a)	you (f.) (m.)		
a'tem	you (plural)		

a'vod (v.)   **a'zov (v.)**

a'vod (v.)	to work; to serve; to worship	b'ayeen tova	with a benevolent eye
avoda	labor; service	a'yef	tired
avoda zara	idolatry	a'yen (v.)	to consider, look into
avoda sh'chora	unskilled labor	a'yom	terrible
a'vor (v.)	to pass by; to review; to transgress	az	strong
		aza	Gaza
avtala	unemployment	azaka	alarm, siren sound
avuka	torch	a'zal	sold out
avzem	buckle	azhara	warning
ayara	town	azkara	memorial service, meeting
a'ye? aifo?	where?		
ayeen; aina'yeem	eye; eyes	a'zor (v.)	to help
ayeen ra'a	evil eye	a'zov (v.)	to depart, leave

86

B

ba'akifin	indirectly	bachur	young man; boyfriend
ba'al	husband; master; owner	bachura	young woman; girlfriend
ba'al agala	wagon driver; uneducated man	bad	linen
		badchan	comedian
ba'al ba'yit	landlord, householder	baheer	clear, bright
		bakbuk	bottle
ba'al cha'yeem	living creature; animal	bakee	expert
		bakasha	request; application
ba'al emtsa'im	man of means		
ba'al kishron	talented person	bain	between, among
b'al korcho	against his will	bainteyem	meanwhile
ba'al koreh	Torah reader (in synagogue)	bain'le'umi	international
		bainonee	mediocre, average
b'al pe	by heart (memorized)	bai'ur	explanation
ba'al m'lacha	artisan, craftsman	bama	stage, platform
		bana'ee	builder
ba'al mum	invalid, cripple	bairur	clarification
ba'al nisayon	experienced person	bait-avot	old age home
		bait-charoshet	factory
ba'al t'feela	cantor (in synagogue service)	bait-choleem	hospital
		bait-din; bait-mishpat	court (of law)
ba'al tshuva	penitent; newly-observant Jew	bait-do'ar	post office
ba'avur	for; on behalf of	bait-havra'a	convalescent, rest home

87

bait-kafe	coffee shop	b'cheeya	crying, weeping
bait-keesai	toilet	b'cheenam	free (of charge)
bait-kele	prison	b'chol ofen	anyway
bait-k'neset	synagogue	b'chol zot	nevertheless
bait-m'lacha	workshop	b'deecha	joke
bait-olam	cemetery	b'deedut	loneliness
baitsa	egg	boded(a)	lonely (m.) (f.)
bait-sefer	school	b'deeka	examination,
bait-yetomeem	orphanage		inspection
barak	lightning	b'deeyuk	exactly
barbur	swan	beena	understanding
baree	healthy	beera	capital city; beer
b'ree-ut	health	begued	garment
la-b'ree-ut!	gezundheit!	behala	panic
baruch	blessed	belem	brake
barur	clear, evident		(on vehicle)
barvaz	duck	ben	son; child
barzel	iron	ben-adam	human being;
basar	meat, flesh		solid person
basees	basis, foundation	ben-ba'yit	frequent house
bashel	ripe		guest
ba-shel (v.)	to cook	ben-b'rit	fellow Jew (son
bat	daughter; girl		of covenant)
batel (v.)	to cancel	ben-dod	cousin
batlan	loafer	ben-gueel	of the same age
batsal	onion	ben-zug	half of couple;
batu-ach	certain; secure,		mate
	safe	b'erech	approximately
ba'ya	problem	berech	knee
ba'yit	house, home	berez	faucet
b'chasha'ee	secretly	beten	abdomen
b'chavana	on purpose	beton	concrete
b'cheerot	elections	b'fumbee	in public

bifneem   **b'zol**

bifneem	within, inside	boker	morning
bifrotrot	in detail	bor	pit (in ground)
bifrat	particularly	bosem	fragrance
b'hechlet	certainly	boser	unripe fruit
bidur	entertainment	boten	peanut;
bikoret	criticism		pistachio nut
bikur	visit	bots	mud, mire
bikvi'ut	regularly	b'racha	blessing; greeting
bilvad	merely, only	b'raicha	swimming
bilbul	confusion,		pool, pond
	disarray	b'raira	alternative
bimkom	instead of	b'ratson	willingly
bim'yuchad	especially	b'rosh	cypress
bin-rega	immediately	b'rogez	angry; not on
biryon	hooligan		speaking terms
birtsifut	continuously	b'sitonut	wholesale
bishul	cooking	b'sorot	news
b'ita	kick	b'tai'avon	bon appetit!
bitachon	security;	b'tashlumim	installment
	confidence		payments
bitna	lining	b'toch	within
bitu-ach	insurance	b'tsimtsum	sparingly
bizbuz	waste	b'tula	virgin (girl)
b'karov	soon	buba	doll
b'kitsur	briefly	bul	postage stamp
b'koshee	with difficulty	busha	shame; shyness
b'lee	without	bursa	stock exchange
b'lee'a	swallowing	b'vadeye	of course!
b'mikre	by chance	b'vakasha	please; you're
b'meshech	in the course of		welcome
b'nogai'a	with regard to	b'vat achat	all at once
boguer	adult; graduate	b'yoker	expensive
	(of)	b'zol	inexpensive,
bo'hen	big toe; thumb		cheap

CH

chabala	sabotage	chail-sheeryon	armored corps
chablan	terrorist	chail-yam	navy
cha'bek (v.)	to embrace	chailev	fat, grease
cha'ber (v.)	to join, connect, add; to compose	chairum	emergency
		chairut	freedom
		charuts	diligent
chacham	sage; wise person; rabbi (among some Jews)	cha'yat	tailor
		cha'yeel	strength, power; army
		challa	Sabbath, holiday bread
chad	sharp, acute		
chadal (v.)	to cease	chalav	milk
chadash	new	chalavee	dairy dishes
chadashot	news	chalak	smooth
chadeesh	modern	chalal	space, hollow
chadar-shena	bedroom	chalameesh	flint
chadraneet	chambermaid	chaleefa	suit
chafatseem	belongings, baggage	chaleel	flute
		chaleela!	God forbid!
chag	holiday, festivity	chalom	dream
chagav	grasshopper	chalon	window
chagora	belt, girdle	chaluk	robe, gown
chagueega	celebration	chaluts	pioneer
chaik	lap, bosom	cham, chome	hot, heat
chail-aveer	air force	cham(ot)	father-in-law, mother-in-law (of wife)
chail-ragla'yeem	infantry		

chamas   **chaveeteeya**

chamas	violence	chashasha	anxiety
chamesh	five	chashav	accountant
chamesh-esrai	fifteen	chashev (v.)	to compute
		chashov (v.)	to think
chamee-sheem	fifty	chashmal	electricity
		chashuv	important
chamor	donkey	chatan	bridegroom; laureate; son-in-law
chamtsan	oxygen		
chamuts	sour; assorted sour condiments		
		chateech(a)	handsome man, beautiful woman (slang)
chaneefa	flattery		
chaneeya	parking	chateecha	slice, piece
chanot (v.)	to park	chateema	signature, endorsement
chanut, chenvanee	store, storekeeper		
		chatul	cat
charada	horror, fear	chatuna	wedding
chardal	mustard	chats'a'eet	skirt
charata	remorse, regret	chatsee	half
chareeg	irregular, exceptional	chatseel	eggplant
		chatser	courtyard, yard
chareef	sharp, pungent; witty	chatsevet	measles
		chatsot	midnight
charseena	chinaware; porcelain	chatsotsra	trumpet
		chatsuf	insolent
chasa	lettuce	chavash (v.)	to bandage; to put on hat
chaseed	pious; fan; follower		
		chaval	too bad!
chaseeda	stork	chaveela	bundle, package
cha'ser	absent, missing	chaveeta	omelette
chasha'ee	silence	chaveeteeya	blintz; stuffed omelette
chashad	suspicion		

chaveev	likable, lovable	cheeda	puzzle
chaver(a)	friend (m.) (f.); colleague; member	cheedat-tashbets	crossword puzzle
		cheedak	microbe, germ
chaveevee (also: chabeebee)	darling, beloved, dear one	cheelul	desecration
		cheelul hashem	blasphemy
chavura	group	cheelonee	secular
chaya	animal	cheelukai-dai'ot	disagreements
chayal	soldier		
cha'yeem	life	cheerug	surgeon
l'cha'yeem!	to life! (toast)	cheesh-cheesh	quickly
cha'yeg (v.)	to dial	cheesul	liquidation (sale)
chazak	strong	cheever	pale
chazan	cantor	chee-yuch	smile
cha'ze	chest, breast	chee-yunee	vital, indispensable
chazeer	pig		
chazeeya	brassiere; vest	cheeyuvee	positive, favorable
chazeret	horseradish; mumps		
		che'res	clay
chazor (v.)	to return, revert; to regret	cheresh	deaf
		cherem	excommunication
		cherev	sword
cheder	room, chamber	chermesh	scythe
chedva	joy	cherpa	disgrace
chen	charm, grace	cheshek	desire, longing; lust
chesed	benevolence		
chelkee	partial	cheshbon	arithmetic; account; bill
che'ma	butter		
chemla	compassion	al cheshbon	on account
chet	sin	chevra	society, company, band
cheeba	love, affection		

cheye   **chutspa**

cheye	alive	chovev	lover; amateur
chidush	innovation	chovevan	dilettante
chiguer	lame	choveret	booklet
chipazon	haste	cho'ze	contract
chipus	search	chug	circle, group,
chisachon	savings, thrift		class
chita	wheat	chukee	legal
chitul	diaper	chulsha	weakness
chodesh	month	chultsa	blouse, shirt
chodshee	monthly	chum	brown
chof	shore, coast	chum'tsa	acid
chofesh	freedom; vacation	chumash	one of
ch'ok	law, statute,		Pentateuch's
	decree		five books
ch'ol	sand	chumus	chick pea dish
cho'le, cho'la	sick (m.) (f.)	chupa	wedding canopy
choma	wall (exterior)	chursaf	artichoke
chor	hole	churban	destruction,
cho'ref	winter		annihilation
choshech	darkness	chush (v.)	to sense, feel
chotem	nose	chut	string, cord,
chotemet	rubber stamp,		thread
	seal	chut	spinal cord
choten(et)	father-in-law,	hash'dera	
	mother-in-law	chuts	outside, exterior;
	(of husband)		except
chov	debt	chuts la'arets	outside Israel
chova	obligation, duty	chutspa	impudence

D

dachu'ee	postponed	deguel	flag, banner
dachuf	urgent	dekel	palm tree
daf	page (in book, magazine)	delek	fuel
		delet	door
dag	fish	derech	way; road; method
dag malu'ach	herring	derech erets	good manners
dag m'mula	gefilte fish	de'she	grass, lawn
d'aga	worry	devek	glue
dagan	cereals, grain	deye	enough
dak	thin, fine	deye'sa	cereal, porridge
daka	moment	d'feeka	knock
dal	meager, poor	d'gam	pattern
dam	blood	deguem	model
darkon	passport	dibur	speech; wise saying
darom	south	dika'on	depression (mental)
dat(ee)	religion; religious	dimum	hemorrhage
davar	thing; mailman	dimyon	imagination
da'yag	fisherman	divu'ach	report
dayal, dayelet	steward(ess)	d'la'at	pumpkin
dayan	judge (in religious court)	d'lee	pail
		d'leka	fire, conflagration
de'a	opinion	d'mama	stillness, quiet
deen	law, judgment	d'ma'ot	tears (from crying)
deera	apartment		

d'mut   **d'yo**

d'mut	shape, figure, image	d'ror	freedom
do'ar	mail, postage	dud	boiler; vat
dod(a)	uncle, aunt	dugma	example, sample
dofek	pulse	dugmaneet	professional model (f.)
do'me	similar		
donag	wax	du'see'ach	dialogue
dor	generation	duvd'van	cherry
dov	bear	d'vash	honey
d'rasha	sermon	d'vora	bee
d'reeshat shalom	regards	d'yo	ink

E

echad, achat	one (m.) (f.)	emek	valley
ed	witness	e'mesh	last night
e'da	community, group, congregation	emtsa	center, middle
		emuna	faith, belief; religion
e'dut	testimony	enav	grape
ee	island	enushee	human
eelan	tree	er	awake, alert
eer	city	erech	value, worth
eer-beera	capital city	b'erech	approximately
rosh ha'eer	mayor	er'es	poison
eereeya	municipality	erets	land, country
eesh, eesha	man; woman; wife	erev	evening
		erev Shabbat	Sabbath eve (Friday night)
eeshi'yut	personality	eru'a	event
eguel	calf	erva	lewdness, shame
b'sar eguel	veal		
efes	zero, nothing	esek	matter, affair
efshar	maybe	eser	ten
efsharut	opportunity	esreem	twenty
egoz	nut	esh	fire; flame
egrof	fist	eshkoleet mits	grapefruit
elbon	insult		
elef	thousand	eshkoleeyot	grapefruit juice
alpa'yeem	two thousand	eshnav	small window
elohim	God	eshtaked	last year

et	pen; time
l'et ata	for the time being
ka'et	now
eeton	newspaper
etgar	challenge
etmol	yesterday
etrog	citron
ets	tree; wood
etsa	advice
etsba	finger; toe
eved	slave

evel	mourning
a'vel	mourner
even	stone
even y'kara	precious stone
ez	goat
ezer	assistance
sefer ezer	handbook
ezer k'negdo	helpmate
e'zor	area, region
ezra	help, assistance
ezrach	citizen; civilian

G

ga'ava	pride	ga'on	genius
gaba	eyebrow	garbayeem	socks, stockings
gabeye	synagogue officer		
gader	fence	gareen	seed, nucleus, kernel
gadol	big, large		
gadoosh	replete	garon	throat
ga'e	proud, haughty	garu'a	worse, inferior
gafrur	match (to kindle fire)	garush, g'rusha	divorced (m.) (f.)
gag	roof	garzen	axe
gagon	awning	gas	crude, vulgar
ga'hak (v.)	to belch	gav	back
gaiheenom	hell	k'ev gav	backache
gal	wave (on ocean)	gaven	hue; complexion
galach	Christian clergyman		
		gavoha	tall
galgal	wheel	gazlan	robber
galu'ee	overt	gazoz	soda (flavored)
gam	also, too	g'dood	battalion
gamad	dwarf	g'doola	greatness
gamal	camel	g'leeda	ice cream
gameesh	flexible, elastic	g'looya	postcard
gamguem (v.)	to stammer	go'al nefesh	disgust
gan	garden; kindergarten	gola	diaspora
		golem	robot
gan eden	paradise	goof	body
ganav	thief	goofiya	undershirt

g'oola	redemption, salvation	guer	convert to Judaism (m.)
goomee	rubber	gueshem	rain
goomeya	rubber band	guesher	bridge
goral	fate, destiny	guet	religious divorce (in Judaism)
goy (eem)	gentile (s)		
goozma	exaggeration		
gueebor	hero	guever	male; a man
gueehuts	ironing	guezer	carrot
gueel	age; joy	gueye	valley
gueelu'ach	shave	g'veenah	cheese
gueemla	pension	g'veer	rich man
gueena	small garden	g'veeya	corpse
gueer	chalk	g'veret	Mrs. Ms., miss; lady
gueersa	text; learning; version	g'vool	frontier; limit
guees(a)	brother-in-law; sister-in-law	g'voora	heroism, courage
gueezbar	treasurer	g'yoret	convert to Judaism (f.)
guefen	vine		

H

ha'adeef (v.)	to prefer	hach'shara	training
ha'aleev (v.)	to insult	hachtava	dictation (to
ha'ameen (v.)	to believe		stenographer)
ha'aracha	entertaining	hach'zeer (v.)	to give back
	(guests),	hach'zeev (v.)	to disappoint
	hosting;	hada'dee	mutual
	evaluation	hadar	splendor; citrus
ha'aratsa	admiration,		fruits
	esteem	hadgueesh (v.)	to emphasize
ha'areech (v.)	to evaluate,	hadpasa	printing
	estimate;	hadreech (v.)	to guide
	to appreciate	ha'dur	splendid
ha'ashama	accusation	ha'eer (v.)	to cast light
ha'aveer (v.)	to transfer	hafgana	demonstration
ha'bee'a (v.)	to express	haf'ree'a (v.)	to disturb
ha'beet (v.)	to look	haf'reed (v.)	to separate
hachana	preparation	hafsaka	pause, inter-
hach'ees (v.)	to anger		mission,
hachleef (v.)	to exchange		cessation
hachleem (v.)	to cure,	haf'seed (v.)	to lose
	recover	haf'sheet (v.)	to undress
hachleet (v.)	to decide	hafta'a	surprise
hachma'a	compliment	haftee'a (v.)	to surprise
hachnasa	income,	hagana	defense
	revenue	hagbala	restriction
hachpeel (v.)	to double; to	hagdara	definition
	multiply	hagrala	lottery

hagshama   **hashkee'a (v.)**

hagshama	realization; implementation	ha'mon	crowd, mob
		ha'mo'nee	vulgar, common
ha'gun	decent, honest	hamra'a	take-off (flight)
haguee'a (v.)	to arrive	hamsheech (v.)	to continue
hagueesh (v.)	to serve (food)	ham'teen (v.)	to wait
haidad!	hurrah!	hamtsa'a	invention
haitev (adj.)	well, nicely	hamula	tumult, uproar
hak'cheesh (v.)	to deny	hana'a	pleasure
hakdama	introduction (in a book)	hanacha	reduction (in price); discount
hatsaga	introduction (to a person)	handasa	engineering
hakdeem (v.)	to precede	hanhaga	management
ha'kee (v.)	to vomit	har	mountain, mount
ha'keer (v.)	to recognize		
ha'kleet (v.)	to record (on tape)	har'be	many, much
		ha'ree'ach (v.)	to smell
hak'seem (v.)	to charm, captivate	hargueel (v.)	to accustom
		hargueesh (v.)	to feel, to sense
hak'sheev (v.)	to listen	hargueez (v.)	to provoke, to irk
halacha	Jewish religious law	harpatka	adventure
hal'beesh (v.)	to dress	hartsa'a	lecture
hit'la'besh (v.)	to dress oneself	hasbara	information; explanation
ha'lel (v.)	to praise	hasbee'a (v.)	to satisfy
hale'lu'ya	praise the Lord	ha'seeg (v.)	to obtain
halva'a	loan (money)	ha'seer (v.)	to remove
halveye!	if only…! would that…!	hash'guee'ach (v.)	to supervise
hamlatsa	recommendation	hashkafa	outlook
hamcha'a	check (remittance)	hashkee'a (v.)	to invest

hashkeem (v.)   **hee**

hashkeem (v.)	to rise early	ha'tseeg (v.)	to display,
hashmatsa	defamation		to introduce
hashmee'a (v.)	to utter, declare		(a person)
hash'meen (v.)	to grow fat	ha'tseel (v.)	to rescue
hashpa'a	influence	ha'tseelu!	help!
hashva'a	comparison	hats'hara	declaration
haskala	enlightenment,	hatsla'cha	success
	wisdom	hats'meed (v.)	to attach, link up
haskama	agreement	havchana	distinction,
haskeem (v.)	to agree		discrimination
haspaka	provisions,	havdala	separation
	supply	ha'vee (v.)	to bring
has'ree'ach	to stink	ha'veen (v.)	to understand
(v.)		havra'a	convalescence
has'teer (v.)	to hide	hav'reek (v.)	to shine
hatchala	beginning	hav'reesh (v.)	to brush
hatcheel (v.)	to begin	havtacha	promise
ha'teef (v.)	to preach, orate	ha'yom	today
ha'teem (v.)	to suit, fit,	ha'zee'a (v.)	to perspire
	resemble	ha'zeek (v.)	to harm
hatkafa	attack	haz'keer (v.)	to remind
hat'reed (v.)	to bother	haz'meen (v.)	to invite, to book
hatsa'a	suggestion	he'a'der (v.)	to be absent
hatsaga	performance	he'ara	remark,
	(stage, screen)		comment, note
hatsbee'a (v.)	to vote;	he'ata	slowing down
	to point	he'atsa	hurrying up
hats'cheek	to cause	hech'sher	authorization
(v.)	laughter		(religious)
hatsee'a (v.)	to suggest,	hed	echo
	to propose	he'der	absence
hatsee'da	aside	hee	she

he'eed (v.)	to testify	hish'ta'yech (v.)	to belong
he'eer (v.)	to rouse, wake	hish'ta'zef (v.)	to sunbathe
hefker	lawlessness; ownerless property	hish'to'mem (v.)	to be amazed
hef'resh	difference	his'ta'der (v.)	to manage, make do; to settle in
hefsed	loss, damage		
heg'yonee	logical	his-ta'guel (v.)	to adapt, adjust
hem	they	his'ta'kel (v.)	to stare, look
he'ra'yon	pregnancy	his'ta'ker (v.)	to earn (money)
hereg	killing	his'ta'lek (v.)	to go away, to take off
he'res	destruction		
he'seg	achievement	his'ta'rek (v.)	to comb one's hair
hesped	eulogy, lament		
he'sus	hesitation	hit'a'bek (v.)	to wrestle
he'tek	copy	hit'a'hev (v.)	to fall in love
he'ter	permission; permit	hit'a'kev (v.)	to delay
hevdel	difference	hit'a'klem (v.)	to acclimate oneself
he'vel	vanity; foolishness	hit'a'lef (v.)	to faint
hidur	splendor; adornment	hit'a'mel (v.)	to exercise
		hit'a'men (v.)	to practice
hi'mur	wager, bet	hit'a'mets (v.)	to strive
hi'sha'er (v.)	to remain behind	hit'a'neg (v.)	to enjoy
		hit'an'yen (v.)	to be interested
hish'ta'del (v.)	to try	hit'a'rev (v.)	to interfere; to bet
hish'ta'el (v.)	to cough		
hish'ta'mem (v.)	to be bored	hit'a'tef (v.)	to cover oneself
hish'ta'mesh (v.)	to use, apply	hit'a'tesh (v.)	to sneeze
		hit'a'yef (v.)	to grow tired
hish'ta'tef (v.)	to participate	hit'balbel (v.)	to become confused

hit'ba'yesh (v.)   **hit'ya'ded (v.)**

hit'ba'yesh (v.)	to be ashamed	hit'la'med (v.)	to teach oneself
hit'bo'le'lut	assimilation	hit'lo'tsets (v.)	to joke, banter
hit'chadesh (v.)	to renew oneself	hit'na'dev (v.)	to volunteer
tit'chadesh!	wear it well!	hit'na'gued (v.)	to oppose
hit'cha'rut	competition	hit'na'heg (v.)	to behave
hit'cha'shev (v.)	to consider, ponder	hit'o'nen (v.)	to complain
hit'cha'ten (v.)	to marry	hit'o'rer (v.)	to wake up, arise
hit'cha'yev (v.)	to undertake; to pledge	hit'pa'le (v.)	to wonder, be amazed
hit'ga'ber (v.)	to overcome	hit'par'nes (v.)	to earn a living
hit'ga'le'ach (v.)	to shave oneself	hit'pa'shet (v.)	to spread out
hit'ga'ot (v.)	to boast	hit'pa'te'ach (v.)	to develop
hit'ga'red (v.)	to scratch	hit'pa'ter (v.)	to resign
hit'ga'resh (v.)	to divorce	hit'pa'zer (v.)	to scatter
hit'ga'shem (v.)	to materialize, to be realized	hit'po'rer (v.)	to fall apart, crumble
hit'ka'dem (v.)	to advance	hit'ra'chetz (v.)	to bathe; to wash up
hit'ka'le'ach (v.)	to take a shower	hit'ra'guel (v.)	to get used to
hit'kal'kel (v.)	to become spoiled	hit'ra'guesh (v.)	to become excited
hit'ka'rer (v.)	to grow cold	hit'ra'kez (v.)	to concentrate
hit'ka'rev (v.)	to approach	hit'ra'shem (v.)	to be impressed
hit'ka'shet (v.)	to adorn oneself	hits'ta'er (v.)	to regret
hit'ka'tev (v.)	to correspond	hits'ta'lem (v.)	to be photographed
hit'ko'nen (v.)	to get ready	hits'ta'nen (v.)	to catch cold
hit'la'besh (v.)	to dress oneself	hits'ta'rech (v.)	to be in need of
hit'lach'lech (v.)	to become dirty	hits'ta'ref (v.)	to join
		hits'ta'yen (v.)	to excel
hit'laha'vut	enthusiasm	hit'ya'ded (v.)	to become friends

hit'ya'esh (v.)   **hu**

hit'ya'esh (v.)	to despair, become discouraged	ho'reem	parents
		hosafa	addition, supplement
hit'ya'guai'a (v.)	to grow weary	ho'seef (v.)	to increase
hit'yash'vut	settlement	ho'sheev (v.)	to seat
hiz'dam'nut	opportunity	hotsa'a	expense; removal; publishing (books)
ho'fee'a (v.)	to appear		
ho'kara	esteem; appreciation; price rise		
hora'a	teaching, instruction; directive	hovala	transport
		hu	he

I

i'bur	pregnancy, conception	ir'gun	organization
sh'nat i'bur	leap year	ir'ur	objection, protest
i'chu'leem	greetings	i'shur	approval, endorsement
i'chur	lateness		
i'kar	principle; farmer	ish'puz	hospitalization
i'kuv	delay	i'sur	ban, prohibition
i'lem	mute	i'tee	slow
im	with; if	it'leez	butcher shop
i'ma; em	mama, mom; mother	it'ree'ya	noodle, pasta
in'yan	matter, affair	i'tur	ornament
i'pa'ron	pencil	i'ver	blind person
		iv'rur	ventilation

K

ka'as	anger	kaf	palm (hand); sole (foot); tablespoon
ka'ba'ee	fireman		
kabala	receipt; reception (in hotel); Jewish mysticism	kafots (v.)	to jump
		ka'fuf	bent over
		ka'ful	double; multiplied by...
kabalat-paneem	hospitality		
kabarneet	captain, pilot	kaftor	button; knob; bud
kablan	contractor		
kab'tsan	beggar, pauper	ka'fu	frozen
kach, kacha	thus, so	ka'hal	assembly; audience; congregation
ka'chesh (v.)	to deny		
ka'chol	blue		
kad	pitcher	kahalacha	properly
kada'chat	fevered illness; malaria	kai'tsad?	how?
		kaiva	stomach; digestive system
kadeema!	forward!		
ka'dish	mourner's prayer	kal	easy, simple, light
kadkod	skull	mash'ke kal	soft drink
ka'dosh	sacred	kala	bride; daughter-in-law
ka'dum	ancient		
ka'dur	ball; pill, tablet; sphere	kalevet	rabies
		ka'lot (v.)	to finish; to destroy
kadur-reguel	soccer		
kadur-sal	basketball		

kalkala   **katsefet**

kalkala	economy; maintenance (financial)	ka'rov	near; relative
		b'karov	soon
kal'kel (v.)	to spoil	karov l'...	almost, approximately
kama?	how much? how many?	karpas	celery, parsley
kamee'a	amulet	karsol	ankle
kamtsan	miser	kar'tees	ticket; card
ka'mut	quantity	kar'ton	cardboard
kan	here	karu'a	torn, tattered
kana'ee	zealot, fanatic	ka'ruch	wrapped
kanaf	wing; fender	kar'yan	announcer
ka'nir'e	apparently	kash	straw (for drinking)
kankan	jug, jar	ka'she	hard, severe
ka'not (v.)	to buy	kasheesh	elderly person
kinyan	property, asset	ka'sher	kosher (food); proper, fair
kapara	atonement, forgiveness	kashor (v.)	to tie, to bind
kap'dan	strict, severe person	kat	sect
		ka'taf	bellman
ka'peet	teaspoon	ka'taigor	prosecutor
ka'pel (v.)	to fold	ka'tan	small
kar	cold; pillow	k'tantan	tiny
k'ara	bowl	ka'tef	shoulder
ka'ra'gueel	as usual	ka'tov (v.)	to write
kar'ai'ach	bald	katsar	short
kardom	axe	k'tsar	
ka'reech	sandwich	ru-ach	impatient
karka	soil, ground, earth	katsav	butcher
kar'keshet	intestine	katseen	officer (military)
ka'ron	car (in train); wagon	katsefet	whipped cream

ka'tseer	harvest	keshet	rainbow; bow
ka'tsots (v.)	to cut, chop,		(for arrows);
	reduce		arc
kav	crutch	ketel	slaughter, killing
kavana	intention;	katlanee	lethal,
	devotion		murderous
	(religious)	keter	crown; title
ka'ved	heavy; liver	kets	ending
ka'vod	honor, respect	ketsev	rhythm, rate
kol haka'vod!	good for you!	ketuba	marriage
kavu'a	regular		contract
k'deye	worthwhile	k'ev	pain, sorrow,
keer	wall (interior)		hurt
kees	pocket	kever	grave, tomb
ke'le	prison	keye'tana	summer camp,
kelev	dog		resort
ke'mach	flour	keye'its	summer
kemet	crease; wrinkle	k'far	village
ken	yes; nest	k'fee'ya	Arabic head
ke'rach	ice		kerchief
keren	ray; fund; beam	k'hila	community
kerur	refrigeration,	kib'ud	refreshments
	cooling	kibuts	collective settle-
ke'sef	money; silver		ment; gathering
ke'sef katan	small change	kidush	sanctification;
	(coins)		blessing on
ke'sem	magic,		wine, bread
	witchcraft	kidushin	marriage
mak'seem	magical,	ki'kar	loaf (bread);
	charming		square (plaza)
ke'sher	connection, link	kilya	kidney
b'kesher l...	in reference to...	kim'at	almost, nearly

kim'o'na'ee   **ko'ne**

kim'o'na'ee	retail; retailer	k'nas	penalty, fine
kin'a	envy	k'neesa	entrance
kinu'ee	nickname	k'neset	parliament
ki'nus	assembly,		(Israeli)
	conference	bait k'neset	synagogue
kin'res	artichoke	k'nufiya	gang
kirva	vicinity	ko'ach	power; energy;
kipa	skullcap; dome		strength
kis'ai	chair	kochav	star
kishalon	failure	ko'dem	previously
kishut	ornament	kodesh	holiness
kita	class (in school)	erets	
kitsonee	extreme;	hakodesh	holy land
	extremist		(Israel)
kivun	direction	l'shon	holy tongue
ki'yor	basin, sink	hakodesh	(Hebrew)
k'lal	total; rule	eer hakodesh	holy city
k'lala	curse		(Jerusalem)
k'lapai	toward, against	kof	monkey, ape
k'lee	utensil;	ko'hal	alcohol
	instrument;	kol-bo	department store
	tool	kol	all; voice; sound
k'lai za'yin	arms	bat kol	echo
k'lai zemer	musical	kol echad	unanimous
	instruments	b'kol	aloud
k'lai lavan	linens (bedding)	ko'lel	inclusive, com-
k'leepa	peel, shell		prehensive
k'leeta	absorption	kol'no'a	movie theatre
k'luv	cage	koma	floor, storey
k'muvan	certainly, of	ko'mer	priest, minister
	course		(Christian)
k'naisee'ya	church	ko'ne	buyer, purchaser

HEBREW – ENGLISH DICTIONARY

kon'inut	readiness	k'taifiya	cape (attire)
korban	victim	k'tata	quarrel, spat
ko're	reader	k'teev	spelling
kos	glass (drinking)	k'teeva	writing
ko'shel	faint, failing	k'tovet	address (residence, office)
kots	thorn, splinter		
ko'sher	ability	k'tsat	small amount
ko'tel	wall (outside)	k'tseetsa	cutlet, hamburger
ha'ko'tel	the wall (remnant of Holy Temple site)	kufsa	box, can
		kumkum	kettle
		kupa'ee	cashier
ko'va	hat, helmet	k'veesa	laundry
ko'zev	false	k'veesh	road, highway
k'reetsa	wink	k'vutsa	group, team
k'ruv	cabbage	k'yosk	refreshment/ newsstand
k'ruveet	cauliflower		
k'saya	glove	k'za'yeet	tiny amount

L

lach	moist	lavyan	satellite
lachats	pressure	la'yil	evening, night
la'chud	apart, separate	lail Shabbat	Sabbath eve
lahaka	troupe,		(Friday night)
	ensemble,	laza'zel!	damn! to hell
	band		with it!
lahav	blade; flame	l'chayeem	to life! (toast)
laida	birth; delivery	l'cheesha	whisper
	of child	le'ben	sour milk,
laitsan	clown		yogurt
lako'ach	customer, client	le'chee	cheek
lakot (v.)	to collect	lechem	bread
laku'ee	defective	pat lechem	slice of bread
lama?	why? what for?	lachmaneeya	roll, bun
lamdan	scholar	le'fet	turnip
la'med (v.)	to teach	l'erech	approximately
la'mod (v.)	to learn	le'set	jaw
lamrot	despite	le'shem	opal
l'an?	whereto?	lev	heart
la'os (v.)	to chew	gueelu'ee lev	candor
la'rov	usually,	tov-lev	kind, compas-
	generally		sionate
lashon	language; tongue	leyela	night, darkness
lashon ha-ra	slander	bin-leyelaw	overnight
latosh (v.)	to polish	k'tonet	
lavan	white	leyela	nightgown
lavosh (v.)	to dress	l'fachot	at least

112

l'faneem   **l'vush**

l'faneem	previously	lo	no, not
l'gueema	swallow, sip	lo k'lum	nothing at all
l'hitra'ot	au revoir	l'olam	forever
lichluch	filth, dirt	l'om	nationality
lif'ameem	sometimes	l'umee	national
lifnai	before, ahead of	lo'azee	foreign, strange
lifneem	within	l'shem	for the sake of
liftan	dessert; stewed fruit	lu'ach	calendar; blackboard; schedule
limud	learning; instruction	lul	child's playpen; chicken coop
s'char limud	tuition		
sefer limud	textbook	lulav	palm branch
likud	amalgamation	l'vad	apart, alone
lina	lodging	l'vana	moon
lishka	office	l'vaneem	underwear, lingerie
l'ma'an	for the sake of		
l'mafrai'a	in advance	l'vaya	funeral procession
l'mala	above, on top		
l'mata	below, underneath	l'viva	pancake
		l'vush	attire, clothes

113

M

ma?	what?	ma'a'var	passage, aisle, transit
ma b'chach?	so what?		
ma l'cha?	what's wrong with you?	ma'bada	laboratory
		ma'bat	view, aspect
d'var ma	something, anything	mab'sut	satisfied, happy (slang)
ma'a'chal	food, dish	ma'cha'la	illness
ma'a'fee'ya	bakery	ma'cha'ne	camp
ma'a'leet	elevator	ma'char	tomorrow
ma'a'mad	stance, position, status	macha'ro'zet	necklace
		ma'cha'sha'va	thought
ma'a'mar	article (in publication)	ma'chat	needle
		ma'chavat	frying pan
ma'a'mats	effort	ma'cha'ze	drama, play; spectacle
ma'a'meen	believer		
ma'a'racha	campaign, struggle, battle	ma'chazor	cycle, circula- tion; (Jewish) High Holiday prayerbook
ma'a'rav	west		
ma'a'reech	appraiser	ma'chazor	blood
ma'a'reets	admirer	ha'dam	circulation
ma'a'se	action, deed, event	mach'be'na	hairpin
		mach'ber	stapler
ma'a'see	practical	mach'be'ret	notebook
ma'a'see'ya	fable, fairy tale	mach'laka	class, depart- ment, ward
ma'a'tafa	envelope		
ma'a'vak	struggle	mach'ma'a	compliment

ma'chol	dance	mag'hets	pressing iron
ma'choz	district	ma'gueed	narrator,
mach'san	warehouse		preacher
mach'sheer	tool, instrument,	ma'guen	shield, defender
	appliance	ma'guen	Shield (or Star)
mach'sor	shortage	da'veed	of David
ma'da	science;	ma'ha'lach	gear (in vehicle);
	knowledge		walking, trip
ma'dan	scientist	ma'heer	prompt, swift
ma'daf	shelf	ma'her (v.)	to hurry,
mad'chan	parking meter		to speed up
mad'chom	thermometer	m'a'hev(et)	lover (m.) (f.)
ma'deem	uniform (attire)	mai'mee'ya	canteen
ma'dor	department,	ma'ka	wound, stroke,
	section		disaster
mad'reech	guide,	ma'kak	cockroach
	instructor;	ma'kar(a)	acquaintance
	handbook		(m.) (f.)
mad're'ga	step, stair;	ma'kel	rod, cane, stick
	level, degree	mak'hai'la	choir
ma'du'a?	why?	ma'ko'let	grocery store
maf'te'ach	key; index	ma'kom	place; space;
ma'ga	contact, liaison		site; God
ma'gaf	boot	bim'kom	in lieu of
ma'gal	circle, circuit	m'ma'le	
ma'ga'neet	daisy	ma'kom	substitute
ma'gash	tray	mi'kol ma'kom	in any case
mag'beet	campaign, fund	ma'kor	source
mag'deer	handbook,	m'ko'ree	original
	guidebook	mak'seem	enticing,
mag'eel (adj.)	disgusting		fascinating,
ma'gue'vet	towel		magical

115

ma'lach   **mash'e'va**

ma'lach	angel; messenger; sailor	mar	bitter; Mr.
		ma'rak	soup
mal'bush	clothes	ma'rat	Mrs., Mme.
ma'lai	full	mar'deem	anathestic, soporific
ma'lai ya'meem	old, long-lived	mar'e	vision, view
		y'fai mar'e	handsome (m.)
ma'lai to'fes (v.)	to fill out a form	y'fat mar'e	beautiful (f.)
		m'a'rai'ach	host
ma'lon	hotel	mar'ga'leet	pearl
ma'lu'ach dag	salty	mar'keev	component, ingredient
ma'lu'ach	herring	mar'pe	cure, remedy
ma'mash	really, substantive	mar'pek	elbow
		mar'tef	basement
mama'shi'yut	reality	mar'tse	lecturer
ma'mon	money	mar'vad	carpet
mam'ta'keem	sweets, candy	ma'sa	burden, load
mam'tsee	inventor	ma'sa u'ma'tan	negotiations
mam'zer	bastard	m'cho'neet ma'sa	truck
ma'na	portion, share		
man'ga'non	apparatus; machinery	ma'sach	screen, curtain
		mas'guer	machinist; locksmith
man'guee'na	melody		
man'heeg	leader	ma'shal	example; fable; proverb
mano'a	motor		
m'an'yen (adj.)	interesting	l'ma'shal	for example
man'ul	lock (on door)	mash'ber	crisis
ma'pa	map; tablecloth	m'a'shen	smoker
ma'pa'la	defeat	m'u'shan	smoked (food)
ma'pe'cha	revolution	mash'e'va	pump
ma'peet	napkin		

116

mash'guee'ach	monitor
mash'kan'ta	mortgage
mash'ke	drink, beverage; liquor
mash'keem	early riser
ma'shosh (v.)	to touch
me'shot	oar
mas'ka'na	conclusion
mas'keel	educated person, intellectual
mas'ko'ret	salary
mas'mer	nail, peg, tack
ma'sok	helicopter
mas'peek	enough
mas'rek	comb
l'his'ta'rek	to comb one's hair
ma'sur	devoted, dedicated
m'at	few
mi'ut	minority
od m'at	soon
ma'ta'na	gift
ma'ta'ra	goal
ma'ta'te	broom
mat'be'a	coin
mat'be'a zar	foreign currency
mat'cheel	beginner
ma'te	staff; baton
ma'te'chet	metal
mat'eem	suitable, fitting
ma'teye?	when?

mat'kon	recipe, formula
mat'meed	diligent, industrious
mat'mon	treasure
ma'tok	sweet
mo'tek	darling
ma'tos	airplane
ma'tsa	unleavened bread
ma'tsav	situation, condition
ma'tsav ru'ach	mood
m'ats'ben	irritating, annoying
m'uts'ban	nervous
mats'ber	battery
mats'bee'a	voter
mats'cheek	funny
mats'eel	lifeguard
ma'tse'va	monument, tombstone
ma'tsee'ya	biscuit, cracker
mats'lee'ach	successful
mats'le'ma	camera
ma'tso (v.)	to find
m'tsee'a	bargain
ma'tsa chen	found favor (in eyes of)
ma'tsor	brake
a'tsor! (v.)	stop!
mats'pen	compass
mats'pun	conscience

117

ma'tu'ach   **me'lach**

ma'tu'ach	tense, taut	m'cho'na'ee	mechanic
ma'tun	moderate, prudent	m'chur'ban	rotten, lousy
ma'us	repulsive	m'chu'tan	person related through child's marriage
ma'vet	death		
mav'reg	screwdriver	m'da'bek	adhesive, sticky; contagious
maf'tee'a	surprising		
ma'yeem	water	m'da'ke	depressing, discouraging
ma'zal	luck, fate		
ma'zal tov!	good luck!	m'deena	country
bar-ma'zal	lucky	m'deena'ee	diplomat
maz'keer(a)	secretary (m.) (f.)	m'deen'i'yut	policy
maz'keret	souvenir	m'dura	bonfire, flame
maz'leg	fork	m'du'yak	precise
maz'mez (v.)	to flirt	me'a	hundred; century
ma'zon	nourishment, food	me'ches	customs, duty
		mech'kar	research
m'cha'bel	terrorist, saboteur	mech'tsa'tsa	toothpick
m'cha'ber	author; composer	mee?	who?
m'cha'nech	educator	shel mee?	whose?
m'cha'shev	computer	m'eel	jacket, coat
m'chee'la	pardon, amnesty	meen	sex; classifi- cation
m'cheer	price		
m'cheeron	price list	me'en (v.)	to refuse
m'cho'ar	ugly	meets	juice
m'cho'na	machine	meets ta'puzeem	orange juice
m'chonat k'veesa	washing machine		
m'chonat k'teeva	typewriter	meets esh'ko'li'- yot	grapefruit juice
m'chonat t'feera	sewing machine	mee'yad	immediately
		me'lach	salt

118

me'lech, mal'ka	king, queen	m'fu'nak	pampered
		m'fur'sam	famous
mel'tsar(eet)	waiter, waitress	m'fu'tach	developed
mem'sha'la	government	m'ga'ma	tendency
me'nora	lamp, candelabrum	m'gue'ra	drawer
		m'guee'la	scroll
me'red	revolt	m'ha'guer	emigrant
me'rets	energy	m'han'des	engineer
mer'ka'va	carriage, chariot	m'hu'dar	elegant, fancy
mer'kaz ta'cha'na	center	m'hu'ma	tumult, panic, riot
mer'ka'zeet	central station	m'hu'pach	upside down, reversed
mer'ka'zee'ya	switchboard		
me'rots	race (for runners)	mich'la'la	college
		mich'ni'sa'yeem	trousers
me'ser	message		
me'shee	silk	mich'se	cover, lid
me'shek	farm	mich'tav	letter
met (adj.)	dead	mich'ta'va	desk
metz'ach	forehead	mi'chuts	outside
me'veen	expert	mich'ya	means of livelihood
me'zeg a'veer	weather		
m'fa'guer	retarded, backward	mi'da	measure, degree, trait
m'fa'kai'ach	inspector, supervisor	k'nai mi'da	standard, yardstick
m'fa'ked	commander (military)	mi'dat ha'racha'meem	merciful justice
m'fa'resh	commentator, interpreter	torat ha'midot	ethical code
m'far'nes par'na'sa	breadwinner livelihood	mid'bar	desert, wilderness

mid'ra'cha   **mish'ka'fa'yeem**

mid'ra'cha	sidewalk	mil'cha'ma	war
mid'rash	study; commentary on text	mil'ga	scholarship
		mi'lon	dictionary
bait mid'rash	study house of synagogue	mi'lu'eem	reserve duty
		mil've	loan (money)
mid'rasha	academy, school	mil'yard	billion
mif'al	plant, factory; project, enterprise	min'hag	custom
		min'hara	tunnel
		min'yan	quorum
mif'gash	rendezvous, meeting place	min'zar	monastery; convent
mif'laga	political party	mir'ka'chat	mixture (perfumes, spices)
mif'letset	monster		
mif'ra'seet	sailboat		
mifrats	gulf, bay	bait mir'ka'chat	pharmacy
mig'da'ni'ya	pastry shop		
migrash	plot (of land); site	mir'pa'a	clinic
		mir'pe'set	balcony, terrace
migrash cha'nee'ya	parking lot	mis'a'da	restaurant
		mis'ba'a	tavern, bar
mik'dash	sanctuary, temple	mis'chak	game
bait ha'mik-dash	Holy Temple	mis'char	business, commerce
mik'la'chat	shower	mis'gad	mosque
mik'lat	shelter	mis'gue'ret	frame; scope; limits
mik're	incident		
mik'te'ret	pipe (smoking)	mish'cha	cream, lotion, paste, ointment
mik'tso'a	occupation, vocation; subject		
		mish'ka'fa'yeem	eyeglasses
mik've	ritual bath (in Judaism)	mish'kifai she'mesh	sunglasses
mi'la	word		

mish'kal   **m'la've**

mish'kal	weight	mits'va	religious command; good deed; duty
mish'mish	apricot		
mish'pa'cha	family		
mish'pat	trial; justice, law		
bait mish'pat	courtroom	miv'chan	test, trial
mish'tar	regime	miv'char	selection, choice
mish'tara	police force	mivrak	telegram, cablegram
sho'ter	policeman		
mish'te	banquet, feast	miv're'shet	brush
mis'ken	wretch, pitiable person	miv're'shet shi'neye'eem	toothbrush
mis'mach	document, certificate	miv'ta	accent, pronunciation
mis'par	number	miv'tsa	project, operation
mispara	barber shop	miz'mor	hymn
mis'para'yeem	scissors	miz'non	buffet, refreshment stand
mis'ra	job, position		
mis'rad	office	miz'rach	east, Orient
mi'ta	bed	miz'ron	mattress
mit'bach	kitchen	miz'va'da	suitcase, valise
mit'cha're	rival	m'ka'rer	refrigerator
mit'ka'dem	advancing, making progress	m'ku'bal	conventional, accepted; Kabbalist
mit'na'gued	opponent	m'ku'dash	sacred, consecrated
mit'pa'chat	kerchief; handkerchief		
mit'ra'chets	bather	m'kulkal	spoiled, defective
mitri'ya	umbrella	m'ku'mat	wrinkled, creased
mits'ad	parade	m'la'chu'tee	artificial
mits'pe	watchtower	m'la'fefon	cucumber
mits'ra'yeem	Egypt	m'la've	escort (m.)

m'lee'tsa   **m'ra'guel**

m'lee'tsa	flowery language	mo'ed	holiday, season:
m'leye	inventory		rendezvous
m'na'hel	manager	mo'a'deem	happy holidays!
m'na'tai'ach	surgeon	l'sim'cha!	
m'natsai'ach	victor, winner;	chol	intermediate
	orchestra	ha'mo'ed	days of
	conductor		holiday
m'na'ya	share, stock (on	mo'eel	helpful
	stock	mo'kesh	obstacle
	exchange)	mo'lad	birth; new moon
m'nee'fa	fan (for cooling)	chag	
m'nu'cha	rest, tranquility;	ha'mo'lad	Christmas
	repose	mo'le'det	birthplace,
m'nu'mas	polite		homeland
m'nu'pach	inflated, swollen	mo'neet	taxi
m'nu'se	experienced	monee'teen	fame, reputation
m'nu'tak	disconnected,	mo'rad	slope, incline
	cut off	m'o'ras	engaged; fiance
m'nu'val	corrupt, villain	mo'ra'sha	heritage
m'nu'zal	down with a cold	mo're, mo'ra	teacher (m.) (f.)
mo'a'don	club for festivity	m'o'rer	stimulating,
mo'chek	eraser		awakening
mo'cher	vendor, salesman	sha'on	
mocho'rat	next day	m'o'rer	alarm clock
mo'cho'ra'-	day after	mo'sad	institution
ta'yeem	tomorrow	mo'sha'va	village,
m'od	very		settlement
mo'da	fashion, style	mo'shel	ruler, governor
moda'a	advertisement	mot	rod, pole
mo'dee'een	intelligence	mot'neye'eem	hips
	service;	moz'na'yeem	scale
	information	m'ra'guel	spy

122

m'ra'guesh   **mu'ral**

m'ra'guesh	exciting	m'tar'guem	translator
mur'gash	emotional	m'ta'yel	hiker
m'ra'nen	refreshing	m'to'raf	crazy, mad
m'ro'hat	furnished	m'tsee'ut	reality
m'ru'gaz	angry, irked	m'tsuch'tsach	polished, shiny
m'ru'pad	upholstered	m'tsu'ka	distress
m'ru'tach	boiled	m'tsu'tsa	garish,
m'ru'vach	spacious, roomy		flamboyant
m'sag'seg	prosperous,	m'tsu'yan	excellent
	blossoming	m'tu'gan	fried
m'sa'nenet	strainer, filter	m'tul'tal	curly-haired
m'seela	track (for	m'tum'tam	stupid
	railroad)	mu'amad	candidate (for
m'seema	assignment,		office)
	task, mission	m'u'chad	united
m'shach'ne'a	persuasive,	mu'chan	ready
	convincing	m'u'char	late
m'sha'mem	boring	much'rach	compelled
m'sho'rer	poet	much'shar	capable, qualified
m'shu'mad	convert (from	m'uch'zav	disappointed
	Judaism)	mud'ag	worried
m'shu'ne	strange, odd	m'ud'kan	up to date
m'shu'taf	partner	m'u'kam	distorted
m'so'ra'tee	traditional	muk'dam	early
m'su'bach	complex,	muk'dash	dedicated
	complicated	muk'pa	frozen
m'su'dar	neat, orderly	mul	facing, opposite
m'su'gal	qualified,	mum	blemish,
	suitable, able		deformity
m'su'kan	dangerous	mum'che	expert
m'su'pak	doubtful	m'u'nan	cloudy
m'ta'ken	fixer, reformer	mu'ral	poisoned

mur'gal	inured, accustomed	m'uv'rar	ventilated, air conditioned
m'ur'pal	foggy, overcast	mu'zar	strange, odd
mu'sach	garage, service station	m'va'ker	visitor; critic; inspector
mu'sag	concept	m'va'ker chesh'bo'not	auditor
mu'sar	morals		
m'u'shar	happy; approved	m'vu'cha	confusion, embarrassment
mush'lam	perfect, whole		
mus'mach	authentic, authorized	m'vu'gar	adult, grown-up
		m'yu'chad	special, unique
mu'tar	permissible	m'yu'tar	superfluous, extra
mu'van	understandable		
mu'van me'e'lav	obvious	m'zee'ma	conspiracy, plot
		m'zu'man	cash

124

N

na	please; if you please	nagan	musician
n'aka	groaning	nagar	carpenter
na'al (a'yeem)	shoe(s)	nahar	river, stream
nachal	stream, brook	na'hog (v.)	to drive
nachala	estate, property	ne'hag	driver
nachash	snake	nakneek(eet)	sausage, frankfurter
na'che	disabled, invalid	namal	port, harbor
nach'esh (v.)	to guess, to estimate	n'mal t'ufa	airport
		na'mer	leopard
nachon	correct, right, proper	na'mog (v.)	to melt, to evaporate
nachuts	necessary, required	namuch	low, short, shallow
nadeer	rare, seldom	na'see	president
nadod (v.)	to wander	naseech, n'seecha	prince, princess
nadvan	philanthropist		
na'e, na'va	nice, handsome, becoming (m.) (f.)	nasu'ee	married
		na'teen	citizen, subject (of country)
na'eem	pleasant, pleasing	natosh (v.)	to abandon
na'fol (v.)	to fall	na'tsel (v.)	to exploit
nafal bapach	fell into a trap	navat	navigator
nafal l'mishkav	fell ill	navon	wise person
		nazeer, n'zeera	monk; nun
nafal chalal	was killed in battle	nechama	consolation

nechmad   **no'ach**

nechmad	lovely, cute, delightful	n'dava	donation
neched, nechda	grandson, grand-daughter	n'dunya	dowry
		nichbad	respected, honorable
neches	asset, wealth	nichzav	disappointed
neder	vow	nichnas (v.)	to enter
ne'edar	absent	nid'me	apparently
ne'eman	loyal, faithful; trustee	nifla	wonderful, marvelous
neen	great-grandchild	niftar	deceased
nefesh	soul, spirit	nigun	melody, composition, tune
neguev	south; southern area of Israel		
negued	against, opposite, anti-	nika'yon	cleanliness
		nakee, n'keeya	clean (m.) (f.)
ne'hedar	splendid		
ne'he'ne (v.)	to enjoy, benefit from	nilhav	enthusiastic
		nisayon	experience, effort, experiment
ner	candle		
nes	miracle; banner		
neshef	party, ball	nistar	hidden
neshek	arms, weapons	nitsots	spark
nesher	eagle	nitu'ach	operation (surgical)
net'to	net amount (after taxes)	niv'ze	contemptible
b'ruto	amount before taxes	n'kama	vengeance
		n'kaiva	female, woman
ne'vel	harp, lyre	n'kaivee	feminine
nezek	harm, damage, injury, loss	n'kuda	dot; period; point
n'cheera	snoring	no'ach	convenient, easy, comfortable
n'choshet	copper		

126

no'ash	hopeless, discouraged	no'zel	fluid
nochree	foreign, foreigner	n'shama	soul, spirit
		n'sheecha	bite
nof	panorama, land-scape, view	n'sheema	breathing, breath
no'ra	terrible, awful	n'sheeka	kiss
no'sai	subject, theme; carrier'	n'tee'ya	inclination
		n'tseeg	agent, represen-tative
no'sai'a	traveller, passenger	n'um	speech, address
		n'urim	youthful age
no'tsa	feather	na'ar(a)	adolescent (m.) (f.)
notsree	Christian		
no'vai'a (v.)	flowing	n'vaila	carcass, carrion
et no'vai'a	fountain pen	n'veecha	barking
noy	beauty, ornamenta-tion	n'vu'a	prophecy
		n'yar	paper
		n'zeekeen	damages, injuries

127

O

ochel	food	omed	standing
le'echol (v.)	to eat	omets	courage
od	another; again; additional	ona	season, period; menstrual period
od m'at	soon	o'na'a	fraud
ain od	there's no more	o'neeya	ship, vessel
od'ef	surplus; excess; change (coins)	o'neg	pleasure, delight
of	fowl; chicken	o'nes	rape
o'fe	baker	o'nesh	punishment
ofee	trait, character	or	light; leather; skin
ofek	horizon	o're'ach	guest
ofen	manner	orech	editor; length; duration
ofna	fashion		
of'na'yeem	bicycle	orech-deen	lawyer
of'no'a	motorcycle	oref	nape
o'hed	sympathizer, supporter	oren	pine tree
		o'rek	artery
o'hel	tent	o'rev	raven
okets	sting; sarcasm	orez	rice
olam	world	o'sher	wealth; happiness
olam haba	hereafter	ot	sign; letter (of alphabet)
olam haze	this world		
bait olam	cemetery	o'tek	copy, duplicate
l'olam	forever	o'tsar	treasure; treasury
olamee	universal	o'yev	enemy
olar	pocket knife	o'zen, ozna'yeem	ear(s)
o'le	ascendant; immigrant to Israel (m.)		
		o'zer	helper, assistant (m.)
ole reguel	pilgrim	o'zeret	maid; helper (f.)

P

pa'ot	small infant	pas	strip, stripe; rail
pa'am	time, step, beat	pas'al	sculptor
hapa'am	this time	pas'cha	Easter
meedai		pa'shut	simple, plain
pa'am	occasionally	pat	slice (of bread)
pa'amon	bell	pa'teesh	hammer
pachad	fear	patu'ach	open
pach'ot	less, minus	pa'yis	lottery
pa'gum	defective, inferior	pe'a	earlock
pairush	commentary, interpretation	pe'a nochreet	wig
		peel	elephant
pa'keed	clerk, beaura-crat; official	peesga	summit, climax
		peetsuts	explosion
pa'leet	refugee, fugitive	pe	mouth
pa'neem	face	pe echad	unanimous
az pa'neem	impudent	k'vad pe	tongue-tied
l'faneem	once, in the past	pe'le	miracle, wonder
b'shum paneem	in no way	perach	flower
pantsher	flat tire; mishap	pe'red	mule
pa'ra	cow	pe'rot	fruits
par'des	orchard	pesach	Passover
parnas	communal leader	pe'sel	sculpture; idol
parpar	butterfly	pe'tee	foolish person
par'va	fur	pe'tek	note, message
parvar	suburb	pe'tel	raspberry

129

petsa   **puzmak**

petsa	wound, injury	p'lada	steel
p'gueesha	meeting, appointment	tsemer p'lada	steel wool
pihuk	yawn	p'leelee (adj.)	criminal
pikai-ach	clever	p'leez	brass
pikchee	shrewd	p'neemee	internal
pikpuk	hesitation	p'neye	free time
pi'le'guesh	concubine, mistress	panu'ee	vacant, available; unmarried
pina	corner		
pinkas	notebook, pad, ledger	po	here
		po'el	worker
pi'nuk	pampering	pol	bean
piryon	fertility	po'rets	burglar
pishpesh	flea	poshe'a	criminal
shuk ha'pish'-p'sheem	flea market	p'rakleet	lawyer
		p'ra'ot	riots
pitgam	proverb, adage	p'ratee	private
pit'om	suddenly	p'ree hadar	citrus fruits
pitriya	mushroom	prozdor	corridor
pitron	solution	p'santer	piano
pitsu'yeem	damages, compensation	p'solet	trash, refuse
		p'shara	compromise
pitu'ach	development	p'tsatsa	bomb
pi'yus	appeasement	puch	eye shadow
p'kak	cork, stopper	pumbee	publicly
p'kuda	order, assigned duty, command	pundak	inn, hostel
		puzmak	stocking

130

R

ra	bad, inferior, troublesome	rai'ach	scent
ra'ad	trembling, shaking	raik	empty
		rak	only
ra'af	tile	ra'kefet	cyclamen
ra'al	poison	ra'kevel	cable car
ra'am	thunder	ra'kevet	train, railroad
ra'anan	fresh (food, air)	ra'kod (v.)	to dance
ra'ash	noise	rikud	dance
r'a'yon	interview, appointment, meeting	rakdan	dancer
		ra'kok (v.)	to spit
		ra'ma'ee	swindler, cheat
ra'a'yon	idea	ram'kol	loudspeaker
ra'bo'teye!	gentlemen!	ram'zor	traffic light
rach	soft, tender, gentle	ra'ot (v.)	to see; to understand
rachav	wide, broad	ra'pai (v.)	to cure
rach'ok	far, distant	r'fu'a	medication, cure, remedy
rachmanut	mercy, pity		
rachum	compassionate	raport	traffic ticket
ra'dum	sleepy	ra'sha	evildoer; wicked/ sinful person
ra'ev	hungry		
ra'gueel	accustomed, usual	ra'tov	wet
		ro'tev	sauce, gravy, food dressing
ra'gueesh	sensitive		
ra'gu'a	calm, relaxed	ratu'ach	boiled
rai'a	lung	ratson	wish, acceptance
		s'va ratzon	satisfied

ratsu'ee	desirable	ree'kuz	concentration
ra'u'ee	worthy, deserving	ree'mon	pomegranate; grenade
rav	large, numerous; rabbi; master	rees	eyelash
rav-aluf	lieutenant-general	reeshon	first
rav-pakad	police superintendent	yom reeshon	Sunday
rav-samal	sergeant-major	reetsa	running; run
rav-seren	major	reetspa	floor
ravak	bachelor	reev	quarrel
raveed	necklace	re'fet	barn
ra'ze	thin, slender	re'ga	moment, minute
chalav ra'ze	skim milk	re'guel	foot; festival
r'chilut	slander, gossip	b're'guel	on foot
r'chov	street, avenue	l're'guel	in connection with
r'chush	property, possessions	raglee	infantryman
r'difa	persecution; chase	re'ka	background
re'a	companion	re'mez	hint, indication
rechev	vehicle	re'shet	network, net
r'ee	mirror	re'tsach	murder
reeba	jam, preserves	risha'yon	permit, license
ree'bas	rhubarb	rishteet	retina
ree'beet	interest (on savings, bond)	rishum	registration; impression; trace
reechuts	washing (personal)	rishul	slovenliness; negligence
reegush	agitation, excitement	r'keema	embroidery
		ro'chev	rider, horseman
		ro'chel	peddler
ree'hoot	furnishings	roch'san	zipper

ro'dan	dictator, tyrant	rosh'mee (adj.)	official
ro'esh	noisy		
ro'fe	physician	rov	majority
ro'fe sheena'-yeem	dentist	al pee rov	generally
rofef	weak; loose	ro'va	quarter, section (of area)
roguez	anger	ro've	rifle
b'roguez	on bad terms with...	r'sham'kol	tape recorder
		r'sheema	list
ro'kai'ach	pharmacist	r'shut	permission
rom	height; altitude	r'tsee'nee	serious
rosh	head; chief; start	ru'ach	wind; spirit; air
		r'ut	visibility
rosh memshala	prime minister	k'tsar r'ut	nearsighted
		r'chok r'ut	farsighted
rosh chodesh	new month	r'vacha	comfort
		r'vee'ee	fourth
rosh hashana	New Year	yom r'vee'ee	Wednesday

S

sa'ad	aid, welfare	safsal	bench
saba	grandpa	sa'gur	closed
sa'bal	porter	sak	bag, sack
sa'bon	soap	sakana	danger
sa'char	wages	sa'keen	knife
s'char deera	rent	sa'kra'nut	curiosity
s'char limud	tuition	sa'kum	cutlery (acronym)
maskoret	salary	sal	basket
sa'check (v.)	to play	sa'lat	salad
mischak	game	sam	poison; drug
sa'chakan	actor	sam r'fu'a	medicine
sach ha'kol	sum total	sa'mal	sergeant
	(restaurant	sa'mai'ach	happy
	bill, e.g.)	chag	
sa'chot (v.)	to squeeze	sa'mai'ach!	happy holiday
sachtan	extortionist,	sa'moch (v.)	to support,
	blackmailer		to rely on
sa'chur	hired, rented	sandak	godfather
sa'deen	bedsheet	sandlar	shoemaker
sa'deer	regular	sa'naigor	defense counsel
sadran	usher	santer	chin
sa'fa	lip; language;	sa'pa	sofa, couch
	shore	sa'pan	sailor
s'fat em	mother tongue	sa'par	barber
s'fat yam	seashore	sa'per (v.)	to tell, relate
sa'fam	moustache	sar	minister
sa'fek	doubt		(government);
sa'fog (v.)	to absorb		officer; prince
safran	librarian	sar ha'otsar	finance minister

134

　　　　　　　　　　　　　　　　　　　s'gol

sar hachuts	foreign minister	b'seder	okay
sar habitachon	defense minister	k'seder	regularly
s'ara	storm	see	pinnacle, summit
sa'rev (v.)	to refuse	seecha	conversation;
sarguel	ruler (for		lubrication
	measuring)	seeka	pin
sarguel		seekat	
chishuv	slide rule	bitachon	safety pin
sa'rog (v.)	to knit	seem (v.)	to put, to place
sa'rot (v.)	to scratch	seem lev	pay attention
sartan	cancer; crab	seeman	mark, sign,
sa'son	rejoicing		omen, signal
sa'tum	blocked up;	seen	China
	obscure	seer	pot
sav	grandfather	seera	rowboat
sava	grandmother	sefel	cup
saveev	around, in a	sefer	book
	circle	sefer ezer	reference book
savlanut	patience	sefer tora	Scroll of Law
savol (v.)	to suffer, to	seguen	lieutenant
	carry burden	selek	beet
savov (v.)	to encircle	selek lavan	turnip
savta	grandma	semel	symbol
s'cheeya	swimming	seren	captain; axle
s'chora	merchandise	seret	film; ribbon;
s'chum	amount, sum		tape; stripe
s'dera	boulevard	s'farad	Spain
se'ar	hair	s'fardee	Spanish; Jew
sechel	sense, brains		from Iberia
sechel yashar	common sense		area
seechlee	sensible	s'faton	lipstick
seder	order, arrange-	s'feena	ship, boat
	ment;	s'gol	violet (color)
	Passover meal		

135

s'gula   **s'veeva**

s'gula	virtue; superb traits	so'chen	agent
siba	cause	sochnut	agency
sich'such	dispute	so'cher	merchant, businessman
si'dur	prayerbook (Jewish)	sod	secret
sifree'ya	library	sof	end, finale
sigsug	prosperity; flourishing	sof-sof	finally
		so'fer	scribe; author
sig'non	style	solela	battery
siku'ee	prospect	so'ne	enemy
simcha	joyous occasion; happiness	s'ora	barley
		so'va	satiety
simla	dress (for woman)	s'raifa	fire, blaze
		s'roch	shoelace
simta	alley	s'tam!	for no reason!
si'na	hatred	s'tav	autumn
sin'or	apron	s'teera	contradiction
sipuk	satisfaction; supply	s'uda	festive meal, banquet
sipur	story, tale	su'fa	gale
si'to'na'ee	wholesaler	sufga'neet	donut (jelly filling)
siyum	conclusion, end; school graduation	sug	classification, category
		su'kar	sugar
s'leecha!	excuse me!	su'kareet	artificial sweetener
s'martut	rag		
s'meecha	blanket	su'kari'ya	candy
s'meechut	ordination	su'kot	Feast of Tabernacles
s'mol	left		
s'na'ee	squirrel	su'lam	ladder
s'neef	branch (of company)	sus	horse
		s'veeva	surroundings

SH

sha'a	hour; time	sha'dod (v.)	to rob, to pillage
sha'a ka'la	briefly	sha'fu'ee	sane
l'fee sha'a	for the time being	shag'reer	ambassador
		shak'dan	diligent person
sha'anan	serene	sha'ked	almond; tonsil
sha'ar	gate, entrance	sha'kol (v.)	to weigh
sha'a'shu'a	amusement, entertainment	shak'ran	liar
		sha'lee'ach	messenger; delegate
shabbat	Sabbath (Saturday)		
		sha'lem (v.)	to pay
sha'ber (v.)	to break, to smash	sha'lem (adj.)	whole, complete, safe
she'ver	hernia; fracture, break	sha'lo'ach (v.)	to send
		sha'lom	peace; greeting for hello and goodbye
sha'cha'reet	morning service (Jewish)		
sha'chatsan	arrogant person	sha'lom ba'yeet	domestic peace
sha'chen	neighbor	d'ree'shat sha'lom	regards
shach'nai'a (v.)	to persuade	chas	
sha'cho'ach (v.)	to forget	v'sha'lom!	God forbid!
sha'chor	black	a'lav	may he rest in
sha'chov (v.)	to lie in bed; to be ill; to go to bed with...	ha'sha'lom	peace
		sha'lot (v.)	to govern, to control
shad	breast		
shad'chan	matchmaker	shal'she'let	chain
sha'deye	Almighty		

137

sham   **shem**

sham	there	she'tach	expanse, area
shamash	beadle,	sha'ul	borrowed
	attendant,	sha've (adj.)	be worth;
	caretaker		resembles;
sha'ma'yeem	heaven, sky		be like
sha'men (adj.)	fat (m.) (f.)	shaveet	comet
(sh'me'na)		sha'vot (v.)	to rest
sha'me'net	cream	sha'vu'a	week
sha'mesh (v.)	to serve	sha'yach	belongs; is
sha'mo'a (v.)	to hear		relevant
sham'ran	conservative	sha'yeesh	marble
sha'na	year	sha'zeef	plum, prune
sh'na'ta'-		sha'zuf	tanned
yeem	two years	sh'chee	armpit
sha'na		sh'chu'na	neighborhood
m'u'beret	leap year	she'char	liquor
yom		she'chem	shoulder
ha'sha'na	anniversary	shed	demon, evil
sha'not (v.)	to change		spirit, ghost
shi'nu'ee	alteration, change	sh'eefa	ambition;
sha'ol (v.)	to ask; to borrow		inhalation
sh'ela	question	sheer	song; poem
sh'eela	borrowing	shee'ta	system
sha'on	clock, watch	she'fa	abundance
sha'ov (v.)	to pump, to	she'ker	lie
	draw (water)	ed she'ker	false witness
sha'pa'at	grippe, flu	she'ket	quiet
sha'rav	intense heat	shel(ee)	of; mine
sha'reer	muscle	she'leg	snow
shar'vul	sleeve	she'let	placard, sign
sha'tee'ach	carpet	shem	name; fame;
sha'tu'ach	flat, even		title

138

HaShem   shu'taf

HaShem	God	sh'guee'a	mistake
shem p'ratee	first name	shi'a'mum	boredom
l'shem sha'-ma'yeem	for God's sake; for an ideal	shi'bo'let	ear (of corn)
chi'lul Ha Shem	sacrilege, blasphemy	shi'bo'let shu'al	oats
she'men	oil	shich'rur	liberation
she'men da'gueem	cod liver oil	shich'va	layer, tier
		shid'ra	spine
she'men see'cha	lubricating oil	shi'duch	marital match, betrothal
she'mesh	sun	shi'dur	broadcast, transmission
bain hash'-ma'shot	twilight	shi'ga'on	madness
shen	tooth; ivory	shi'ga'yon	obsession, passion
ro'fe-shi'na'yeem	dentist	shi'gra	routine
she'na	sleep	shi'kor	drunkard
she'reet	remainder	shi'kun	housing development
she'rut	service; shared taxi (jitney)	shil'shom	two days ago
		shil'shul	diarrhea
shesh	six	shim'shi'ya	parasol
shesh es'rai	sixteen	shi'mu'shee	useful
shisheem	sixty	shi'pur	improvement
she'ten	urine	shi'puts	renovation, repair
she'vach	praise, com-mendation	shir'yon chail	armor
she'vet	tribe, clan; rod	shir'yon	tank corps
sheye	gift	shit'chee	superficial
sh'gaga	unintentional error or offense	shi'tuf	partnership
		shi'tu'fee	cooperative
		shu'taf	partner

shi'tuk   **shul'chan**

shi'tuk	paralysis	sho'fet	judge, referee
shi'ul	cough	shok	calf, leg
shi'ur	lesson; estimate	sho'me'a	listener
shi'vu'ee	comparison	sho'mem	desolate, uninhabited
shi'yut	rowing		
sh'lav	phase, stage	sho'mer	guard
sh'leelee	negative	sho'ne	different
sh'leeshee yom	third	sho'resh	root, source
		sho'shan(a)	lily; rose
sh'leeshee	Tuesday	sho'te	fool, madman
sh'mad	forced conversion of Jews	sho'tef	flowing, fluent
		sho'ter	policeman
sh'mar'taf	babysitter	mish'ta'ra	police force
sh'mu'a	rumor	sho'vav	mischievous
sh'neye'eem	two	sh'ree'ka	whistle
pee sh'neye'eem		sh'tar	promissory note
	double		
sh'norer	person living on handouts; parasite	sh'tee'ka	silence
		sh'tee'la	planting
		sh'tee'ya	drinking
sho'a	Holocaust; catastrophe	sha'tu'ee	drunk
		shat'yan	drunkard
sho'chad	bribe	sha'ta	
sho'cher	backer, supporter	l'cha'yeem	offered a toast
		sh'tut	nonsense
sho'chet	Jewish ritual slaughterer	shu'al	fox
		shu'eet	bean
sho'far	ram's horn (sounded during High Holy Days)	shuk	outdoor market; bazaar
		shi'vuk	marketing
		shul'chan	table

shum   **sh'ya'reem**

shum	garlic; nothing	sh'vee'ta	strike (labor)
b'shum	under no cir-	sh'vee'tat	
o'fen	cumstances	ne'shek	armistice
shu'man	fat	sh'vee'tat	
shu'ra	row, line,	she'vet	sitdown strike
	series	sh'vu'a	oath
shuv	again	sh'vu'on	weekly
shuv (v.)	to return; to		publication
	repent	sh'ya'reem	leftovers,
sh'veel	path		remnants

T

ta	cell; cabin; compartment	tachtoneet	lady's slip
ta'am	taste	tachbura	communications; transportation
ta'ana	complaint		
ta'ala	canal; channel; trench	tachboshet	bandage
		tachleet	aim; practicality
ta'alul	prank; mischievous child	tachsheet	ornament; rascal (slang)
		tadeer	frequent
ta'aluma	enigma	ta'eem	tasty
ta'amula	propaganda	ta'ev (v.)	to loathe, to abhor
ta'anug	pleasure		
ta'ar	razor	tafreet	menu
ta'areech	date (calendar)	taguen (v.)	to fry
ta'asuka	employment	tahalucha	procession
ta'arovet	mixture	tahor	pure
ta'arucha	exhibition	tafel	tasteless
ta'areef	charge, fee	tafkeed	task, assignment, duty
ta'aseeya	industry		
tabach (at)	cook, chef (m.) (f.)	tafos (v.)	to catch, to seize; to understand
taba'at	ring	tafus	occupied, taken
tabur(ee)	navel; navel orange	t'aina	fig; fig tree
		tairuf	madness
tachana	station, depot	ta'ur	description
tacharut	competition	taiva	box, crate
tachat	under, below; instead of	tai-avon	appetit!
		b'tai-avon!	bon appetit!
tachtoneem	underwear; men's shorts	tal	dew

talu'ee	depending; suspended; dubious	tamtseet	summary, digest
		tanach	Jewish Bible (acronym)
taleet	prayer shawl	tanur	stove, oven
tal'fen (v.)	to phone	ta'pes (v.)	to climb
talush	detached; alienated; torn off	tapu'ach resek	apple
		tapucheem	apple sauce
t'lush	coupon	tapud	potato
talmeed	student	tapuz	orange
talmeed chacham	scholar	tarbut	culture
		taree	fresh (food)
taltal	curl (hair)	tarmeel	bag, satchel; knapsack
tam	innocent, faultless, simple	tarn'gol	chicken
		tarn'gol hodu	turkey
tam'e	unclean, impure	tarud	busy
tanef (v.)	to befoul	tas	tray
tavo'a (v.)	to drown, to sink	tashlum	payment
tamar	date (edible); date palm tree	tashmeesh	implement
		tashmeeshai k'dusha	ritual articles
takala	mishap, failure	ta'ut	mistake
takeen	regular, normal	tayar	tourist
takeef	strong, resolute	tayas	pilot
takleet	record (for listening)	ta'yel (v.)	to take a walk
takreet	incident	tayelet	promenade, esplanade
taktseev	budget		
tameed	always	tazkeer	memo
ner tameed	Eternal Light (in synagogue)	t'chelet	blue, azure
		t'cheela	beginning
tameem	naive	t'cheeya	revival, renaissance
tamruk	cosmetics		

t'chum	border; range; limit	tifrachat	rash
t'chusha	sensation, feeling	tiltul	wandering
teechon	central	`tikra	ceiling
yam teechon	Mediterranean Sea	tikva	hope
		tikun	repair, reform, improvement
bet sefer teechon	high school	tilboshet	clothing
teek	file, brief case, portfolio	tipa	drop, small amount
teel	missile, rocket	tipesh	foolish person
teemahon	amazement	tipul	care (for another), attention, treatment
teenok	infant, baby		
teeras	corn (edible)		
teesa	flight	tipus	type, kind
teev	characteristic, quality	tipusee	typical
		tircha	special effort
tee'yul	trip, outing, walk	tirda	bother
teker	flat tire	tirgul	practice, drilling
tekes	ceremony	tirgum	translation
tel	mound, pile, knoll	tisporet	haircut
		tizmoret	orchestra
te'red	spinach	t'kufa	period, age, season
te'va	nature		
teevee	natural	t'leye	patch
te'vach	massacre	t'luna	complaint
tevel	condiment, seasoning	t'muna	picture, photo, image
t'feela	prayer	t'neye	condition
t'guva	reaction	al t'neye	conditional
t'heela	praise, splendor	t'na'eem	betrothal ceremony
tiferet	beauty, glory, honor	t'nu'a	movement, motion; traffic

144

t'nuch	lobe	to'shav	resident; inhabitant
t'nuva	produce, yield		
toch	within, interior, center	totsa'a	result
		to'tseret	product
tochen	contents	tov	good; kind
tochneet	program, plan, project	tova	favor, good deed
		tovala	transport
toda	thanks; gratitude	tovai'a	prosecutor; plaintiff
toda raba!	thank you very much!		
		t'raif	non-kosher food
to'e	mistaken	t'raisar	dozen
to'elet	usefulness, benefit	t'raklin	living room, parlor
to'en	plaintiff, claimant	t'rees	shutter; thyroid
tof	drum	t'reet	sardine
tofa'a	phenomenon	t'rufa	medicine, remedy
toferet	seamstress		
tofes	copy, sample	t'ruma	donation, gift
toladot	chronology	t'shuva	repentance; reply; return
toldot cha'yeem	curriculum vitae		
		tubin	cookie
tomaich	supporter, backer	t'ufa	flying, aviation
t'omeem	twins	n'mal t'ufa	airport
tor	line, queue; column; turtle	t'uda	document, certificate
torah	Pentateuch (first third of Jewish Bible)	t'udat ze'hut	identity card
		t'vee'a	claim, demand
sefer torah	Scroll of Law	t'vu'a	crops, grain, produce
to'rem	donor		
tosefet	increase; supplement; addendum	t'zuna	nutrition; diet
		t'zuza	movement, motion

TS

tsa'ad	pace, step	tsa'me	thirsty
tsa'ar	sorrow	tsameed	bracelet
tsabar	cactus; native-born Israeli (sabra)	tsamud	linked, attached
		tsanchan	parachutist
		tsanu'a	modest, humble
tsach	pure	tsa'ok (v.)	to shout
tsa'chok (v.)	to laugh	ts'aka	outcry
tsad	side; aspect	tsar	narrow
ba'tsad	nearby	tsara; tsa'rot	trouble; misfortunes
tsadeek	righteous person; pious; just		
		tsar lee	I'm sorry
		tsarchan	consumer
tsa'eef	veil, scarf	tsar'edet	hoarseness
tsa'eer	youth; young	tsa'reech	necessary, needed
tsafon	north		
tsa'fuf	crowded	tso'rech	necessity, requirement
tsa'fun	hidden		
tsahal	Israel Defense Force (acronym)	ain tso'rech!	there's no need!
		tsa'ref (v.)	to combine, attach to; add
tsa'hov	yellow		
tsala'chat	plate, dish		
tsalam	photographer	tsa'revet	heartburn
tsa'leket	scar	tsa'rud	hoarse
tsa'lot (v.)	to grill, to roast	tsava	army
tsa'lu'ee	roasted, grilled	tsavar	neck
tsaltsel (v.)	to phone; to ring up	tsavaron	collar

tsa'yad	hunter	tsilum	photograph
tsedaka	charity;	tsimuk	raisin
	generosity	tsinor	pipe (plumbing)
tse'da	supplies,	tsi'peet	pillow case
	provisions	tsipor	bird
tsedek	justice	tsipo'ren	nail (on finger,
tsee	fleet, navy		toe); carnation
tseer	envoy; axle	tsitut	quotation,
tsee'yun	mark; indication,		citation
	note	tslav	crucifix, cross
tsee'yur	painting,	ts'leel	sound, tone
	illustration,	ts'meeg	tire (on vehicle)
	drawing	ts'non	radish
tsel	shade; shadow	ts'o'fe	spectator; scout
tse'mach	plant, vegetation	tso'ho'la	rejoicing
tseemcho'nee	vegetarian	tso'ho'reye'-	
tsemed	pair, couple	eem	noon
tsemer	wool	aruchat tso'-	
tsemer	absorbent	ho'reye'eem	lunch
guefen	cotton	tso'lelet	submarine
tse'va	color; paint	tso'met	junction
tsevet	crew	tsor'fat	France
ts'fardai'a	frog	ts'reef	shack, hut
tsi'bur	public;	tsur	boulder, rock;
	community		fortress
bri'ut		tsura	form, shape
ha'tsi'bur	public health	ts'veeta	pinch
yachasai		ts'vee'ut	hypocrisy
tsi'bur	public relations		

U

uchlusee'ya	population	um	U.N.
uga	cake		(acronym)
uguee'ya	cookie	uma	nation
ugav	organ (musical)	u'man	artisan
u'lam	hall, auditorium	umlal	wretch; pitiable
uleye	perhaps		person
ulpan	studio; intensive	umtsa	steak
	study	uvda	fact

V

va'ad	committee	vav	hook, peg
va'ada	commission	v'eeda	convention
vada'ee (adj.)	certain, sure	veedoo'ee	confession
valad	new-born infant	veeku'ach	debate
vareed	vein	vee'lon	curtain, drape
varod	pink	vee'tur	renunciation,
va'ter (v.)	to concede		surrender
va'teek	senior, veteran	vered	rose (flower)

148

Y

yahadut	Judaism	yam	sea, ocean
yahalom	diamond	yameen	right (direction)
ya'ar	forest	yam teechon	Mediterranean Sea
yabelet	blister		
yachad	together	yanshuf	owl
yachas	attitude	yarai'ach	moon
yachef	barefoot	yarchon	monthly (publication)
yachol	capable		
yachsan	high-born, haughty person	yarech	thigh
		yareed	market place, fair
yad	hand; memorial	yareev	adversary
yada	cuff	yarok	green
yadeed	close friend	y'rakot	vegetables
yadeet	handle	yashan	old (objects)
yadoo'a	famous	yashar	honest, upright
ya'eel	effective, efficient	yasheer	direct, non-stop
		yasheesh(a)	old man (woman)
ya'eh (adj.) (n.)	seemly, fitting; shovel	yashen	asleep
		yashvan	buttocks
yafe, yafa	beautiful, lovely (m.) (f.)	yateret	appendix (anatomy)
yagai'a	tired, weary	yatom	orphan
yagon	sorrow	yatseev	stable
yakar	precious; expensive	yatseg (v.)	to represent
		yavan	Greece
ya'kee'ree	dear one, beloved	yavesh	dry
yalda	small girl	ya'yeen	wine
yalkut	satchel, small bag; anthology	y'dee'a	information, knowledge

yee'poo'eeko'ach   **y'vool**

yee'poo'ee-ko'ach	power of attorney	yitron	advantage, gain
yeera	fear, awe	yizkor	memorial service
ye'led	small boy, child	yo'ets	advisor
yehudee (adj.) (n.)	Jewish; Jew	yo'fee	beauty
yeter	excess, remainder	yom	day
ye'tser	impulse, inclination	yom chameeshee	Thursday
		yom reeshon	Sunday
		yom r'vee'ee	Wednesday
ye'ush	despair, hopelessness	yom shainee	Monday
		yom sheeshee	Friday
ye'reeda	descent		
ye'reeka	spitting	yom shleeshee	Tuesday
yesh	there is, there are	yoman	diary
yesh lee	I have	yom-yomee	ordinary, routine
yesh l'cha?	do you have? (to a male)		
		yo'na	dove, pigeon
yesh lach?	do you have? (to a female)	yo'resh	heir
		yo'shev rosh	chairman
yeshiva	meeting, session; religious school	yo'sher	honesty, integrity
		yo'ter	more
		yovel	jubilee, anniversary
yeshu'a	salvation		
yesod	foundation, basis	yozma	initiative
yetsee'a	exit; departure	y'sureem	suffering
y'faifeh, y'faifee'ya	extraordinarily handsome (m.) (f.)	y'tsoo	export
		y'tsoor	production, manufacturing
yishuv	settlement	y'voo	import
yi'ta'chen	possible, maybe	y'vool	crops, yield

Z

zach	pure	zeek	spark
zachar	masculine	zeekaron	memory
zahav	gold	zeelzul	scorn,
zaban(eet)	salesman,		disrespect
	saleswoman	ze'hut	identity
za'eer	tiny	zer	wreath
zaheer	careful	ze'ra	seed
zagag	glazier	ze'ret	pinky (little
za'kan	beard		finger)
za'ken	old, aged	z'ev	wolf
za'kuf	upright, erect	ze'vel	manure;
zakuk	in need of		garbage
zamar;	singer (m.) (f.)	z'man	time
zameret		z'manee	temporary
zameer	nightingale	zol	cheap,
zanav	tail		inexpensive
zar	foreign, alien	zohar	glow,
za'reez	agile, adroit,		brightness
	alert	zo'na	prostitute
zarkor	projector,	zoog	pair, couple
	searchlight	zoo'yaf	fake, forged
zarnuk	hose (for water)	zooz (v.)	to move, to stir
za'yeet	olive	z'reecha	sunrise
ze'a	perspiration	z'reeka	injection,
z'chucheet	glass (for		throwing
	window)	z'ro'a	arm, forearm
z'chut	privilege, right	z'vuv	fly

Phrases Frequently Used by Visitors

Sha'lom   *Hello or goodbye (literally, peace)*

Sha'bat shalom   *Good or peaceful Sabbath*

Bo'ker tov   *Good morning*

Lei'la tov   *Good night*

Le'hi'ra'ot!   *Au revoir!*

Ma shlom'cha (m)   *How are you?*

Ma shlomaich (f)   *How are you?*

Ma nishma?   *How's everything?*

Kacha, kacha   *So, so*

Mazal tov   *Congratulations*

L'cha'yeem!   *To life! (a toast)*

B'va'kasha   *Please*

Al-lo-davar   *It's nothing (You're welcome)*

S'leecha   *Excuse me*

Lo m'da'ber eevreet   *(I) don't speak Hebrew*

M'dabreem angleet?   *Does one speak English?*

Na, l'at l'at   *Please, slowly*

Od pa'am   *Again*

Na, lichtov zot   *Please, write it*

Kama ze o'leh?   *How much does it cost?*

Re'ga b'vakasha   *One minute, please*

B'se'der   *It's okay*

Y'meena   *To the right*

S'molah   *to the left*

Yashar, yashar   *straight ahead*

Maspeek   *It's enough*

Yo'ter   *More*

Pa'chot   *Less*

Ma'hehr   *Quickly*

Yo'ter m'oochar   *Later*

A'nee m'maher (m)   *I'm in a hurry*

A'nee m'maheret (f)   *I'm in a hurry*

Kar lee   *I'm cold*

Cham lee   *I'm warm*

Ain lee moosag   *I haven't a clue*

Ma zeh?   *What's this?*

Ai'fo zeh?   *Where is it?*

Ha'eem pa'too'ach?   *Is it open?*

Lo me'veen   *I don't understand*

Tachanah mer'kazeet   *Central bus station*

Aizeh otoboos no'say'ah l...?   *Which bus goes to ...?*

A'tah maguee'ah l...?   *Do you go to...?*

Ka'mah ha'ne'see'ah?   *How much does the trip cost?*

Na, l'hagueed lee ai'fo la'redet.   *Please tell me where to get off.*

B'vakashah l'hazmeen mo'neet.   *Please call a taxi.*

Ka'mah z'man zeh yikach?   *How long will it take?*

A'tzor po, b'vakashah   *Please stop here*

Cha'keh lee   *Wait for me*

Ain lee kesef katan   *I have no change*

Ma hachesh'bon?   *How much is the bill?*

Aroo'chat e'rev   *Dinner*

Aroo'chat tso'ho'rei'yeem   *Lunch*

Mee sham?   *Who's there?*

B'vakashah, yesh tafreet b'angleet?   *Do you have an English menu, please?*

Ai'fo yesh mis'adah tovah?   *Where is there a good restaurant?*

Ma'yeem ka'reem   *Ice water*

A'nee tzo'reech ro'feh   *I need a doctor*

Do'ar aveer   *Air mail*

Michtav rashoom   *Registered letter*

Efshar lishlo'ach mivrak?   *Can I send a cable?*

Ha'derech b'teekoon   *The road is under repair*

Ha'eem zot ha'derech l...?   *Is this the way to ...?*

Ma ha'sha'ah b'vakashah?   *What time is it, please?*

Ain lee z'man, slee'chah   *Excuse me, I have no time*

A'nee ro'tseh karteeseem   *I want tickets*

Ma'tei matcheela ha'hatsaga?   *What times does the show start?*

Ha'eem efshar l'hachaleef kesef zar lishka-
   leem?   *Can I exchange foreign money to (Israeli) shek-
   els?*

A'nee rotseh l'hit'kasher ....   *I want to contact ....*

Ma h'sha'ot shelachem?   *What are your hours?*

Ha'eem yesh hartsa'ot b'angleet?   *Are there lectures in English?*

Ha'eem moo'tar l'ta'yar l'vaker
   bak'nesset?   *May a tourist visit the K'nesset (Israel's parliament)?*

Ma h'hevdel bizman bain Yisra'el vinoo
   york?   *What's the time difference between Israel and New York?*

Aifo efshar l'ga'hetz simla/chaleefa
   ma'her-ma'her?   *Where can I get a dress/suit pressed in a hurry?*

Ma'tei sogreem ha'chanoo'yot b'yom
  sheeshee?   *What time do the stores close on Friday?*

Aifo yesh sa'par?   *Where is there a barber?*

Aifo yesh misparah?   *Where is there a hairdresser?*

Anee rotseh l'hodot lachem b'ad kol
  ha'ezrah   *I want to thank you (pl.) for all your help*

Tee'hi'yeh baree!   *Be well! (to man)*

Neh'heh'nai'tee mai'habeekoor seh'lee.   *I enjoyed my
  visit.*

Todah rabah!   *Thank you very much!*

Judaica Titles

1,301 QUESTIONS AND ANSWERS ABOUT JUDAISM
David C. Gross

David C. Gross has expanded his bestselling *1,201 Q & A about Judaism*, a Book of the Month Club selection, with 100 more questions and answers. The author is a former editor of *The Jewish Week* (New York) and is America's premier author of Jewish works, including over 17 titles.

"Ideal for busy people seeking ready answers on the basic questions . . .the amount of information packed into this one volume is amazing."
—Union of Hebrew Congregations

"A kaleidoscopic vision of the rich heritage of Judaism."
—Rabbi Norman Lamm,
President, Yeshiva University

448 pages   6 x 9   0-7818-0578-3   W $17.95pb   (678)

UNDER THE WEDDING CANOPY: LOVE AND MARRIAGE IN JUDAISM
David C. Gross and Esther R. Gross

This comprehensive book delves into the wide range of marriage customs, ceremonies, traditions, and practices, that have become part of the Jewish heritage for nearly four thousand years. David Gross and his wife, Esther, have spent years assembling material that will shed new light on the vast, complex world of Jewish marriages.

"An ideal gift for couples . . .practical, full of useful information."
—*The Forward*

"Jewish wedding customs from around the world…advice on how to creatre a happy marriage."
—*American Jewish World*

"A portrait of Jewish marriage that is unfailingly positive and unabashedly traditional."   —*Na'amat*

243 pages   5 ½ x 8 ¼   0-7818-0481-7   W $22.50hc   (596)

DID THE CHILDREN CRY?: HITLER'S WAR AGAINST JEWISH AND POLISH CHILDREN
Richard C. Lukas

Winner of the 1996 Janusz Korczak Literary Competition for books about children.

"…[Lukas] intersperses the endless numbers, dates, locutions, and losses with personal accounts of tragedy and triumph…A well-researched book…"   —*Catalyst*

263 pages   15 b/w photos, index   0-7818-0242-3   W $24.95hc   (145)

YOUR LIFE IS WORTH MINE

Ewa Kurek; with an introduction by Jan Karski

The story, never told before, of how Polish nuns in World War II saved hundreds of Jewish lives while risking their own. First published in Poland as Gdy Znaczyl Zycie in 1992, this long awaited American edition includes a section of interviews with nuns and Jewish survivors which did not appear in the Polish edition.

"A welcome addition to Holocaust literature...deserves a wide readership."   —*Zgoda*

"The subject of Polish nuns saving Jewish children is a very fascinating one. The author gives us great insight into the many complexities involved."   —*News of Poland*

250 pages   0-7818-04094 $22.50hc   W   (240)

WHY REMAIN JEWISH

David C. Gross

"He shares practical information for getting involved in Jewish life."
        —*The Jewish Week*

171 pages   0-7818-0216-4 $9.95pb   W   (213)

JEWS IN POLAND: A DOCUMENTARY HISTORY

Iwo Cyprian Pogonowski

This classic historical work describes the rise of Jews as a nation and the crucial role that the Polish-Jewish community played in its development.

402 pages   maps/illustrations/index   8 ½ x 11   0-7818-0604-6 $19.95pb   (677)

FORGOTTEN HOLOCAUST: THE POLES UNDER GERMAN OCCUPATION, 1939-1945 (REVISED EDITION)

Richard C. Lukas; Foreword by Norman Davies

This new edition includes the story of Zegota and the list of 700 Poles executed for helping Jews.

300 pages   6 x 9   illustrations   0-7818-0528-7   W $24.95hc   (639)

DICTIONARY OF 1,000 JEWISH PROVERBS

David C. Gross

This multilingual collection of 1,000 Jewish proverbs is extracted from the rich oral traditions of Hebrew, Yiddish, and Aramaic, and has been edited with both the scholar and the general reader in mind. Covering a wide range of topics, the proverbs reflect lives whose spiritual abundance often contrasted a material impoverishment.

The transliterated and translated proverbs are arranged by Hebrew subject; a complete index in English accompanies the text.

131 pages   5 ½ x 8 ½   0-7818-0529-5   W $11.95pb   (628)

JEWISH FIRST NAMES

David C. Gross

Names for the 21ˢᵗ Century for boys and girls, based on traditional, biblical, historical, and contemporary sources.

128 pages   5 X 7   0-7818-0727-1   W $11.95hc   Spring 1999

TREASURY OF JEWISH LOVE

128 pages   5 x 7   0-7818-0308-X   W $11.95hc   (346)

Dictionaries

ENGLISH-ROMANIZED HEBREW/ ROMANIZED HEBREW-ENGLISH COMPACT DICTIONARY

157 pages   3 1/8 x 4 5/8   7,000 entries   0-7818-0568-6   W $7.95pb   (687)

EASTERN ARABIC-ENGLISH/ ENGLISH-EASTERN ARABIC DICTIONARY AND PHRASEBOOK

(for the Spoken Arabic of Jordan, Lebanon, Palestine/Israel and Syria)

This book provides the traveler to the Eastern Mediterranean with a practical aid for communicating in Arabic. It is based on the spoken language widely understood in Jordan, Lebanon, Palestine/Israel and Syria. A brief description of Arab grammar and a pronunciation guide is followed by 2,200 entries of useful and up-to-date phrases and basic key vocabulary with an intentionally easy-to-use pronunciation system in English spelling. Phrases cover all topics a traveler needs to know including numbers, transportation, shopping, eating out and much more.

220 pages   3 ¾ x 7   2,200 entries   0-7818-0685-2   W $11,95pb   (774)